WRITING FOR RAKSMEY

WRITING FOR RAKSMEY

A STORY OF CAMBODIA

JOAN HEALY

© Copyright 2016 Joan Healy
All rights reserved. Apart from any uses permitted by Australia's Copyright Act 1968, no part of this book may be reproduced by any process without prior written permission from the copyright owners. Inquiries should be directed to the publisher.

Monash University Publishing
Matheson Library and Information Services Building
40 Exhibition Walk
Monash University
Clayton, Victoria 3800, Australia
www.publishing.monash.edu

Monash University Publishing brings to the world publications which advance the best traditions of humane and enlightened thought.

Monash University Publishing titles pass through a rigorous process of independent peer review.

www.publishing.monash.edu/books/wr-9781925377125.html

Series: Investigating Power
Series Editor: Professor Clinton Fernandes, UNSW Canberra at the Australian Defence Force Academy

Design: Les Thomas

Cover: (left to right) Srey Leik, Monee, Nee, Reaka (as a new born baby), Yeay, Raksmey. Ruin of Khmer Monastery Battambang Province near the Sankei River. Photographs by Scott Rankin, 1993.

National Library of Australia Cataloguing-in-Publication entry:

Creator:	Healy, Joan, author.
Title:	Writing for Raksmey : a story of Cambodia / Joan Healy.
ISBN:	9781925377125 (paperback)
Subjects:	Healy, Joan.
	Cambodia--History--20th century.
	Cambodia--Social conditions--20th century.
	Refugees--Cambodia.
Dewey Number:	959.6

Printed in Australia by Griffin Press an Accredited ISO AS/NZS 14001:2004 Environmental Management System printer.

The paper this book is printed on is certified against the Forest Stewardship Council ® Standards. Griffin Press holds FSC chain of custody certification SGS-COC-005088. FSC promotes environmentally responsible, socially beneficial and economically viable management of the world's forests.

CONTENTS

Acknowledgements vii
Preface viii

PART I: TELLING ABOUT THE CAMP 1

1	Writing for Raksmey	2
2	Thai-Cambodia Border, 1989	9
3	Into the Life of It	16
4	Crossfire	25
5	Ta Phraya	34
6	Healing	45
7	Birth	49
8	Pain	52
9	CPR	55
10	Samsara	60
11	To See inside Cambodia	70
12	Facing the Fear	77
13	The Beginning of the Ending	84

PART II: THE RETURN 97

14	Back to Cambodia	98
15	Out of Town	107
16	A Home	116
17	Khmer Way	119
18	Noticing	124
19	Election Year	128

20	Ansang Sok, Spean, Chroy Ampor, Wat Kundung	142
21	Facing Reality	150
22	The Year that Drew Us Backwards	155
23	Two Families	165
24	Spanning the Distance	174

PART III: BRINGING BACK THE STORIES **185**

25	The King Father is Dead	186
26	Sok Thim	192
27	Theary	198
28	Nee	201
29	Battambang	207
30	Touern	211
31	Krom	215
32	Peou and Thalika	217
33	Phaly and Soeun	221
34	Raksmey	225
35	Ratanikiri	227
36	Ieng Sary and Kieu Samphan	230
37	Struggles and Tensions	234
38	2014	238
39	Ka	240
40	Lum Aung	246
41	Proan Pra	248
42	The Farm	255
43	The Light Shines Through	257

Sources and Further Reading 261

ACKNOWLEDGEMENTS

I acknowledge Cambodian friends whom I first met behind barbed wire on the Thai/Cambodia border. Their friendship has remained strong during more than a quarter of a century; they have trusted me with the narrative of their lives.

I thank Maria Tumarkin: teacher, friend, mentor and gifted writer. Her belief sustained my own conviction that a story such as this must be written. Maria's readiness to inspire, challenge and encourage has been vast.

My family, my friends and my religious community, the Sisters of St Joseph, have supported me throughout the labour of writing. Some gave back letters I had sent from Cambodia, some read and reacted to drafts. They surely know that I am grateful.

Through the responsiveness of many people, this narrative has become a book.

PREFACE

Beginning in the first month of 1979 Cambodians in their thousands stumbled towards the border of Thailand, the only place they could hope to find refuge. They were emaciated and afraid. Some carried children in their arms or on their backs; injured people were pushed in handcarts. By May the Red Cross was feeding forty thousand refugees. Journalists and photographers from across the world jostled for stories and filed reports of torture, slave labour and executions.

Survivors told of three years, eight months and twenty days of terror, of family members lost or killed. They described Cambodia, smaller in area than Victoria, as littered with the bodies of victims. Careful calculation has now shown that almost a quarter of Cambodia's population of between seven and eight million had suffered 'forensic death', death caused by crime. The Communist Party of Kampuchea, CPK, known as the Khmer Rouge or Red Cambodians, had held the total population captive. While this was happening the attention of the world media was elsewhere.

It was 17 April 1975, just before the North Vietnamese troops entered Saigon, that the army of the Khmer Rouge reached Phnom Penh. There were no longer government troops to oppose them. The population, swollen by refugees from battles in the countryside, awoke to silence instead of to the familiar sound of war. At sunrise young Khmer Rouge soldiers, some clad in black pyjamas, some in tattered army uniforms, were noticed on the streets. For years government troops had been fighting the Khmer Rouge. It was as if peace had come at last. As the sun rose higher on this hot April morning families cheered and girls brought flowers.

PREFACE

By noon the young fighters began issuing orders from their leaders for the entire population to leave their homes and evacuate to the countryside. The evacuation was chaotic but the intention of the Khmer Rouge leadership was purposeful.

Family members who were in different parts of the city when the command was given were separated without farewell. Patients were pushed on trolleys from the hospital wards and even from operating theatres. The elderly, the disabled, the very young, the mothers giving birth and those who questioned the command were the first to die. The purpose of this exodus of people forced to walk north, south, east or west away from Phnom Penh was, in the mind of the Khmer Rouge leaders, the very-great leap forward, the re-founding of Cambodia/Kampuchea. The nation was to emerge as a pure communist state.

The leaders were a circle of young Cambodians who had been sent to France for post-graduate study and had returned, most with doctorates, all with a dream for change. There was in Paris a Cambodian section of the French Communist Party convinced that revolution was the way to free their country from a long history of despotic leadership, corruption, impunity, greed and oppression of the poor. Back in Phnom Penh they worked as teachers, university lecturers, or politicians seeking opportunities to influence others. Saloth Sar, later known as Pol Pot, had failed his exams. He began working in rural villages for the CPK.

This ferment took place during the reign of Norodom Sihanouk. For centuries Cambodians had been ruled by monarchs with absolute power. The French, who had established a Protectorate over Cambodia, appointed Norodom Sihanouk as King in 1941. He was a self-described playboy with an ebullient personality; they expected him to be their puppet. As it happened he claimed glory for gaining independence from France, resigned as King, appointed his father in his place and assumed a role of 'head-of-state'; in this way gaining more power. His was a one-party regime that lasted until 1970. He cultivated international relationships and gained aid to spend on health and education. By the end of the sixties the number of children in school had increased by 400 percent and there were opportunities for the brightest to pursue post-graduate degrees overseas. He later ruefully said that he should have been more careful about this. He spent time among peasant farmers offering small gifts to their families. They saw him as the God-King and called him King Father. Activists and even members of his cabinet who dared to have a view different from his risked torture and execution. A significant number fled to the jungle to join the communists.

The first small Cambodian communist cells in the 1950s were inspired and supported from North Vietnam. During the late 50s the intellectuals from France abandoned their careers in the city one by one and gained leadership within the CPK. They had a vision of a rural-based, simple society. City dwellers would be re-educated by the labour of working the land, a hard life that would teach simple values. People who could not adjust would die. This would remedy the suffering inflicted by vast inequalities of wealth and power. It would be a classless society.

The program to train revolutionaries blended the Cambodian culture in which they themselves had been shaped with the communist theory that they had absorbed in Paris. Among them were men who had lived and been taught in Buddhist monasteries during their schooldays, as was common in Cambodia. In their communist movement, as in familiar Cambodian monastic tradition, detachment and renunciation were central. For a worthy society to be brought

PREFACE

about, it was taught, one must be ready to sacrifice, to renounce possessions and renounce family. The planned revolution would create a nation where all people were equal and would work together for the common good. For this great goal they should detach their hearts from feelings of guilt or hesitation about tough actions that must be taken. This could be understood even by recruits who were illiterate. It was repeated like the mantra of the monks; it was 'correct behaviour'. Earnest young people and disillusioned activists were taught to sacrifice everything for this revolution.

A central theme of the indoctrination was loyalty to every aspect of the party's policy and organisation. There was rigid hierarchy and a code of secrecy. Like teachers in the traditional schools the leaders wrote the rules that adherents to the organisation must obey. Those who would renounce everything in personal life and be willing to kill even their mother or father for the cause of the revolution could expect to be highly regarded.

Pol Pot, who became leader of the CPK in 1962, was adamant about the need to root out enemies. The more zealous followers responded by 'smashing the enemy' through ritual torture that had been known in Cambodia for centuries. Zealous Khmer Rouge cadre would do a 'wild' thing to restore 'correctness'. One example, practiced by some Khmer Rouge though not only by them, was to tie an enemy to a tree, cut out his liver and as he died cook and eat it. This demonstrated that the revolutionary was detached of heart, and able to kill without wavering. In addition the eating of liver would bring courage to the liver of the one who ate it for the liver was the seat of courage. Admiration was gained by brutalising an enemy until he was no longer human.

WRITING FOR RAKSMEY

The Khmer Rouge movement would have dwindled and disappeared as did other extreme groups in earlier times, but a series of events nobody could have foreseen swelled its ranks until it became a force to be taken seriously. Both the policies of the USA and the unpredictable decisions of Norodom Sihanouk strengthened the Khmer Rouge. Though Norodom Sihanouk did not set out to support the communists, and successive Presidents of the USA feared communism and set out to eradicate it, the Khmer Rouge gained supporters from their actions.

Sihanouk made choices to maintain ties with neighbouring countries and with the international community. While America and its allies were supporting the South in the war in Vietnam, the National Liberation Front, known as the Viet Cong by Western sources, ferried munitions through Cambodian and Laotian territory. Sihanouk chose to ignore this, navigating relationships with the USA, the Soviet Union, North Vietnam, France, South Vietnam and the USSR simultaneously. The Viet Cong nurtured the fledgling Cambodian communists, the Khmer Rouge, in the jungle areas that they shared, until 1970.

Between 1965 and 1968 President Johnson began bombing attacks on Cambodian territory. The Khmer Rouge fanned the anger of rural Cambodian populations who suffered from these attacks. In March 1969, as part of his strategy to end the Vietnam conflict, the newly elected President Nixon ordered intensified bombing. 'I want anything that flies to go in there and crack the hell out of them. There is no limitation on mileage an there is no limitation on budget. Is that clear?' Nixon's National Security adviser, Henry Kissinger, relayed the order: 'A massive bombing campaign in Cambodia.

PREFACE

Anything that flies on anything that moves.' Recruitment for the Khmer Rouge escalated in rural areas.

Sihanouk, mainly because he now believed the North Vietnamese would overcome the South, cut off relationships with the USA. His decision was disputed by the Cambodian military commanders, who depended on American aid, but Norodom Sihanouk did not brook dispute; in January 1970 he set out on a journey to Paris, Moscow and Peking seeking financial support. Before he reached Peking he was usurped as leader by Lon Nol, who was pro-American. The Chinese leadership supported the Khmer Rouge. Sihanouk was persuaded to become the movement's 'titular head'. The former King broadcast by radio into Cambodian villages to strengthen armed resistance against Lon Nol. This appealed to rural populations where he was still regarded as King Father. It also further boosted Khmer Rouge recruitment.

Nixon, to take attention away from US withdrawal from Vietnam, ordered carpet bombing across eastern Cambodia and closer to Phnom Penh. During the American raids 2,765,941 tons of bombs were dropped on Cambodia, compared to 2,000,000 tons dropped by the allies during the whole of Word War Two, including the bombing of Hiroshima and Nagasaki. The US Congress, in response to protests of US citizens, cut off funds for the bombing of Cambodia in August 1973. This left Lon Nol's army without aerial support. The Khmer Rouge army was already strong; the fall of Phnom Penh was inevitable.

Phnom Penh fell to the Khmer Rouge in 1975.

On seizing power the Khmer Rouge declared Year Zero. They abolished private ownership, abolished currency, closed markets, schools and monasteries, and emptied towns. Townspeople were sent to rural areas where they would labour without pay and without rights to build a nation that the Khmer Rouge named Democratic Kampuchea.

Sihanouk was flown back from China to become Head of State, to represent Democratic Kampuchea internationally and to ensure a seat for this 'new nation' at the United Nations General Assembly in New York. He achieved these tasks with his usual ebullience, but a short time after his return to Phnom Penh he resigned from his role, pleading health problems and the need to travel to China for medical treatment. The leadership denied his request and kept him under 'house arrest'.

By the end of the first year of their regime the Khmer Rouge identified 'failures' preventing the revolution from reaching its goals. They suspected sabotage and disloyalty. Purges of 'the guilty' commenced. All, even senior Khmer Rouge officials, lived in fear. Suspicion became paranoia, torture yielded new names of traitors. Bodies rotted in fields and Buddhist Wats and schools became torture centres. In Toul Sleng, the largest of these prisons, more than twelve thousand prisoners were photographed, tortured until a confession was extracted, and then executed. Khmer Rouge interrogated mercilessly, in the 'correct way'.

The regime was nationalistic, obsessed about safeguarding Cambodia's borders and regaining territory lost to neighbouring Vietnam, Laos and Thailand. Border areas were attacked without provocation. The Vietnamese, backed by the Soviet Union, timed their response carefully.

Late in 1978 the Vietnamese army advanced towards Phnom Penh along the highways that converged on the capital. They were well armed and equipped and in two weeks 'liberated' the country.

PREFACE

Pol Pot, now recognised as Khmer Rouge Brother Number One, announced resumption of guerrilla warfare from the jungles.

The Vietnamese Communist army reached Phnom Penh on 7 January 1979 and installed a regime, to be known as the People's Republic of Kampuchea, with a governing body of Cambodians appointed and advised by Vietnamese. Its leaders and many of its members had fought with the Khmer Rouge before defecting to Vietnam in 1977–78. A twenty-three year old former Khmer Rouge commander, Hun Sen, became the Minister for Foreign Affairs. In 1985 Hanoi appointed him Prime Minister.

Millions who had been held captive by the Khmer Rouge walked the roads seeking food and freedom, seeking lost family members, seeking their former homes, or seeking safety at the Thai border. Those who clustered close to Thailand were a mixed group, of deserters from the Khmer Rouge army, peasant farmers, former business people, intellectuals, artists, black marketeers and other opportunists, as well as many widows and children.

Civilians were a magnet for international aid and resistance groups made their bases close by, where they were supported by foreign allies. The Chinese resurrected the Khmer Rouge army. The USA, Western powers, and ASEAN states supported two anti-Communist resistance groups, the Khmer Peoples National Liberation Front (KPNLF) and the United Front for an Independent, Neutral, Peaceful and Cooperative Cambodia (known by its French initials, FUNCINPEC). The USSR supported the Vietnamese troops stationed in Cambodia. This force attacked the resistance; the resistance attacked back with logistical help from the Thais. Many of the refugees caught in the crossfire realised that they were being used as political pawns.

WRITING FOR RAKSMEY

After two years of sheltering in China, Sihanouk agreed to lead a national front, consisting of the two non-communist resistance groups together with the Khmer Rouge. It was named the Coalition of Democratic Kampuchea and occupied the seat at the United Nations previously held by the Khmer Rouge.

In 1989 the USSR withdrew support from Vietnam. The Vietnamese troops, having trained and armed a military force for Prime Minister Hun Sen, withdrew from Cambodia. Within two years Peace Accords were signed in Paris.

A United Nations Transitional Authority for Cambodia (UNTAC) governed beside a Supreme National Council (SNC), consisting of representatives from each of the four factions. Sihanouk presided over this. The border camps were closed and more than three-hundred-thousand people were brought back into the country, to a doubtful future. The Khmer Rouge refused to demobilise as agreed in the Accords, withdrew from the planned election, and continued fighting. They held territory in Battambang Province and mined gems and cut timber to trade for armaments. UNTAC Peace Keepers were blocked from entering their territory. Hun Sen boosted the numbers of his powerful national police by moving soldiers into this force instead of demobilising them. He refused to allow UNTAC to oversee them. The Khmer Rouge continued their war until 1998, holding a 'liberated zone' and threatening villages and towns.

Four million people voted in the 1993 General Election. FUNCINPEC gained the majority of votes but Hun Sen rejected the outcome. After a standoff and the threat of further bloodshed Sihanouk proposed that, for the sake of national reconciliation, there would be a coalition government with two Prime Ministers: Ranariddh the leader of FUNCINPEC and Hun Sen the leader

PREFACE

of the CPP. Hopes for the stability of the Peace Accords and for democracy faded.

When the compromise disintegrated in 1997 Hun Sen emerged as sole Prime Minister, the role he had held from 1985. The United Nations Commission for Human Rights and other human rights groups filed thick documents detailing political and civil rights abuses under his leadership.

Early in Hun Sen's leadership I stood in the foyer of a restored reception centre in Phnom Penh, waiting for a conference to begin, talking among a small cluster of people that included the Prime Minister. During the conversation he commented that without his strong authority there would be far more bloodshed. He believed it.

Hun Sen's power mirrored that of despotic Cambodian rulers before him. He had ultimate control over the judiciary, the armed forces, the police and secret security teams. Journalists and editors with opposing views were assassinated and nobody was ever found guilty of their deaths. Before each election there were political murders.

The Paris Agreements had not provided for accountability for Khmer Rouge crimes but had simply called for a 'non-return to the policies and practices of the past'. In the late 1990s Hun Sen agreed to negotiate with the United Nations for a tribunal; one set up on his terms. It was now generally accepted that the Khmer Rouge regime was responsible for between 1.7 and 2.12 million deaths. In Western countries there was a public call for the perpetrators of the Khmer Rouge atrocities to be held accountable. The United Nations General Assembly, against the advice of the Secretary-General, eventually agreed to a tribunal formula acceptable to the Prime Minister. Western countries, including Australia, were willing to provide the funding needed for a court to proceed on Hun Sen's terms.

WRITING FOR RAKSMEY

A compromise was agreed. The Extraordinary Chambers in the Courts of Cambodia (ECCC), established in 2001, would comprise a minority of judges and co-prosecutors nominated by the UN Secretary General, and a majority of judges and co-prosecutors selected from the Cambodian judiciary and appointed on the approval of Hun Sen. The period to be examined would be precisely the days of the Khmer Rouge regime; nothing earlier, nothing later. The ECCC would try 'senior Khmer Rouge leaders' and those 'most responsible'.

Pol Pot had died in the jungle in 1997.

Kaing Guek Eav, aka Duch, the commander of Toul Sleng Interrogation Centre, and Ta Mok, known as the Butcher of Battambang, were already in prison. Ta Mok died there.

Hun Sen gave permission for the police to apprehend Noun Chea, Pol Pot's deputy, Khieu Samphan, president of Democratic Kampuchea from 1976 until 1979, and Ieng Sary, a co-founder and senior member of the Khmer Rouge and foreign minister and deputy prime minister of Democratic Kampuchea from 1975–79, together with his wife Ieng Thirith. Ieng Sary died in prison before coming to trial; his wife was assessed as not fit to be tried because of advanced dementia.

Case 001, the trial of Duch, sifted through a vast number of documents and called many witnesses even though the accused admitted guilt. People from the countryside were bussed to Phnom Penh to watch. Duch was sentenced to life imprisonment.

Case 002, the trial of Noun Chea and Khieu Samphan, had both men appear together because they were already elderly and frail. Pressure was mounting for more convictions before further suspects died. Khieu Samphan in particular protested against this, saying that his role was quite different from that of his co-defendant. Many

PREFACE

aspects of this case left grounds for appeal and in mid-2015 the court was still bogged down in hearing appeals.

Hun Sen, his appointed judges and the police have refused to co-operate with any further trials. Trial 003 could bring evidence from the Eastern Zone where Hun Sen and Chea Sim, a senior member of Hun Sen's government, held positions of authority. Many former Khmer Rouge members and military leaders have official roles in Cambodia's present government.

Despotic leadership, corruption, impunity, greed and oppression of the poor prevail now as they did when the Khmer Rouge leadership first shaped their vision of Year Zero. Corruption remains an unchecked problem. The gap between rich and poor is extreme. Crimes are committed with impunity and people are imprisoned without cause. Powerful elites plunder the nation's resources. Land is 'grabbed' from the poor and sold to big companies for profit. I have seen all of this. There is an oft-repeated Cambodian proverb: 'The rich plough the backs of the poor'.

Ω

In writing this necessary background I have turned to historians and other scholars whom I trust. I acknowledge them as my source. There is however a parallel narrative. It tells of ordinary women and men in Cambodia, and of their response to these grim times. Theirs is a story about compassion, courage and humour. Goodness persists. Whether it sprang from the dark tangle of Cambodia's past, or simply survived it, I cannot say.

I must write about this because I have seen it, and know. There is beauty: a terrible beauty.

Part I

Telling about the Camp

1

WRITING FOR RAKSMEY

'I know my father better than he thinks I do,' he says. The dust of the road rises through the broken window of the car and through the cracks where the door latch is loose. We taste dust, stop talking. The traffic tangles; it slows to the pace of walking. This lanky, dusky young man with his high cheekbones and large almond eyes exudes the confidence of the newly well-educated as he navigates it all. I watch his hands on the steering wheel, relaxed as he steers through a chaos of early morning motorbikes, pushbikes and tuk-tuks. His are strong, dark hands, like his father's hands.

Drivers lean on their horns. No chance and no need for me to say 'I knew your father before you were born.' He knows that.

I count the years: it must be twenty-three years since he was born in a tiny makeshift shelter in the refugee camp. A little scrap of life lucky to survive. That day in 1989 the shelling between the Cambodian army and the Cambodian resistance was heavy and close to the camp.

On the day he was born his father asked, 'Do you think his skin is too dark?' and revealed the burden of a man whose walnut-brown skin would always mark him as of peasant-farmer stock. His mother said, 'My husband will never be dead while this boy is alive. They are exactly the same.'

WRITING FOR RAKSMEY

Today the north road to Battambang from the Cambodian capital Phnom Penh is surging with life; girls on the way to the garment factories dart between motorbikes loaded with passengers, with goods, with pigs and chickens in cane baskets.

A tight circle of locals is forming at the edge of the road. Drivers turn off their engines; they and their passengers crane to see through the dust and the throng, some shouting suggestions, children held aloft. An accident? A vendor of traditional medicine? Something more sinister?

A gap forms like a tunnel through the knot of vehicles. Raksmey veers into the opportunity: he rides the curb, left wheels on the embankment, right wheels to the road, one hand clamped firmly on our loudest of all horns, the other gripping the steering wheel, knuckles ridged. We break free of the pack, swerve to our proper side of the road and head into clear highway between rice fields. 'Tell me about the camp,' he says, looking ahead to the pale line of hills.

'What do you want to know Raksmey?'

'Everything,' he replies.

It will be four or five hours before we reach Battambang. There is time. He waits, I weigh and sift all that I know, then plunge into the heart of his story.

'It was a crowded camp with barbed wire all around it and Thai military guards. There were almost two-hundred-thousand Cambodians behind this barbed wire. Your dad was not much older than you are now. Rations were short; for each person three-and-a-half kilos of rice per week and one small tin of tuna donated by the Japanese, seven litres of water a day for cooking, washing, drinking, bathing, cleaning. People would cook their rice and fish carefully, a little at a time, outside their own shelter, being vigilant to make the firewood ration last. It was a war zone. Your mother was young and very beautiful; the most beautiful woman in the camp, your father told me. They were both delighted when you were born. They chose your name to mean "burst of light".'

Raksmey reaches for a cassette, pushes it into the slot, presses the play button, turns up the volume. Traditional music builds to a crescendo; it wails. We reach the outskirts of a small town. He turns off the music and stops the car, then we walk into a wayside 'restaurant' without talking. He settles me at a table and joins the throng of travellers crowding around the servery, all competing to order a meal. I look around. It's familiar: crowded dining room, cement floor awash with water and litter, cement tables and stools, dead exotic wild animals hanging on hooks ready to be rendered into stew or soup, steaming vats of pre-cooked food, many men and some women each holding the place at a table or shouting an order. I see no other white or pink face. There is the stench of an overflowing squat toilet with a door that will not stay shut.

$$\Omega$$

The conversation has unsettled me. Did I say too much? These distant memories compete with the present as I sit alone minding our table, waiting for Raksmey to bring the food.

It was '88 when I made my first visit to the border of Cambodia. From Bangkok to the refugee camp beyond Aranyaprathet was a long bus journey. There was a 'comfort stop' where vendors below the bus window shouted their wares, peeling green mango on a stick with a twist of paper holding ground chili and sugar for dipping. As

WRITING FOR RAKSMEY

I stepped down from that bus I smelled the stench of an overflowing squat toilet with a door that would not stay shut. There were flies.

During that first visit to Site 2 one small corner of that crowded camp snared my attention. Phaly, the Cambodian refugee woman who created it, told me it was a 'Centre for Healing of Heart and Spirit'; officially it was known as Khmer People's Depression Relief, KPDR. In response to the great sadness this was a brave attempt to offer respect and understanding. For days I sat in that centre: listening to the cadence of the conversations between helper and helped; smelling the pungent healing herbs offered as tea, lotion or balm; watching the stroking, the massage, the gentle soothing.

Crowds of refugees, the sad and the mad with sadness, found shelter here. Phaly invited me to stay as a friend-with-knowledge. There was something in my background that she thought would be useful. At first the idea of staying was preposterous but my meeting with the women and men and children of Site 2 troubled me; blotting this from my mind was impossible. Within months I returned to stay. Those early days are far in the past.

I look towards Raksmey, who threads his way back to the table, balancing steaming plates of rice and vegetables garnished with a little meat. He grins. He is starting to piece the past together. I am piecing the past together too. There is a web of stories more complex than he could ever guess.

He places the bowls carefully on the bare cement table and sits facing me. 'Thank you Smey,' I say. I make no promises, though I am already thinking that back in Australia there could be notes and photographs of those times to pass on to him.

Ω

From as early in my life as I can remember I have scribbled words on paper when sad or glad or puzzled or in awe. I usually burn these pages or tear them up. In the years when I first worked side by side with Cambodians I used thick little notebooks and ballpoint pen. Later I used a typewriter and, as the years went by, a laptop.

That first laptop was black. It was linked with alligator clips to a truck battery which could be balanced on the back of a motorbike and recharged on a generator in a village on the road to Banan. In the heat the shiny black case of this weighty laptop peeled off, revealing silver paint. The silver paint flaked off, revealing a translucent white case. Nevertheless the laptop continued to do what it was meant to do; it accepted and held many words.

During the past quarter-century there have been a lot of words.

$$\Omega$$

Back in Australia, in our Footscray convent, we have a tall storage cupboard. It is a place to search for things that have not been sighted for years. I am hunting for anything I have written that might have details that Raksmey would want to know. Some empty suitcases and travel bags are stacked here, covered with a rug to protect them from dust. I am looking for a China Air bag that may have some old journals in it.

The bag is here. It is as I remembered it: luminous green and yellow. I bring it to the back veranda where winter sun gives more light, then tip the contents onto the mat: a heap of battered notebooks and hard-covered journals, letters, maps, newspaper clippings, my laminated camp-pass and photos. All a bit musty.

WRITING FOR RAKSMEY

Saying farewells to friends has always been difficult for me: goodbye on leaving Australia and goodbye on leaving Cambodia. During the years, after spending many months in one place or the other, I have left on a one-way ticket. No wonder these scraps and relics have been kept. It was hard leaving this time. When my life of 'home-in-two-places' began I was a couple of years over fifty; now I am nudging towards eighty. There will be an end to this; it is inevitable. Love stretched across oceans is as taut as the skin of a ripening mango.

I make a plunger of coffee and settle into a cane chair. It is a relaxed Saturday afternoon. Just outside the glass door pansies bloom in a planter-box, brightening a patch of bitumen, sunlight translucent through magenta-coloured flowers. I'm listening to jazz on the ABC.

There are three or four fat journals that fit the timeframe of the Site 2 Camp; others are from the longer time in Cambodia. I begin to read.

Even before I sift the papers I know that what is written here is intimate; there are stories I could only write because of being trusted. What should be done with all of this? Ought I type from those scribbled pages? Is it too personal to be retold? Years ago these journals and letters could have been cleared away but it's too late now to burn and tear. There are stories that ought to be handed on when another generation is ready to listen. The great-grandparent generation, the Cambodians who lived through the terror of the sixties and seventies and eighties, know this. So do I.

Here there are details I had forgotten. The day of Raksmey's birth is recorded; there is even a photo of the newborn child in the camp. These things should be his, not mine. There are many things here that Raksmey deserves to know and, perhaps, stories that others should know too.

WRITING FOR RAKSMEY

Before I close the journals it is almost dark on the back veranda. The music has stopped; I didn't notice. The coffee is cold.

That border camp of decades ago is not just geography and history. It changed lives: all of our lives changed utterly.

2

THAI-CAMBODIA BORDER, 1989

I stand at a corner in Ta Phraya waiting for the minibus to take me to the camp. Within months of the '88 visit I have returned as a volunteer with the Jesuit Refugee Service. There wasn't much sleep last night and I am finding it difficult to remember what has motivated me to come back.

I stand at the corner with my identification pinned to my tee-shirt. My pass is stamped and signed in Bangkok, and signed again in Aranyaprathet – still eighty kilometres from Site 2. The United Nations Border Relief Operation requires this. So do the Thai authorities. All permissions are in place.

This feels more like dream than reality. I am awkward, gawky. The 1988 visit was only that: an exposure for a limited time. My life, where I live, is now in this place, though it is as if I am in the wrong skin here.

The bus comes; there is nothing to do other than to board it. We are crammed together, volunteers from many nations. There are introductions. Rice fields and small clusters of Thai houses are lit with early sunshine as we pass. The first glimpse of the high fence and barbed wire of the camp jolts me into reality. As we stop at the entrance armed Thai guards check our passes and search the bus. It is the wet season; I am hot and wet already though the day is just beginning.

This is a place of detention. There are only two ways to enter it: as a foreigner with a stamped pass or as an asylum-seeker finding a track through the minefield, crawling under the fence to immediately be detained. Thailand has not signed the UN Refugee Convention; these asylum-seekers are illegal immigrants.

Through the gates is the bamboo-and-thatch city of mud in the wet season, dust in the dry season. From my reading I know that in the flimsy temporary dwellings there are enough women, children and men to populate a small city, at least one-hundred-and-fifty thousand, though the numbers given are never precisely reliable. More than half are children.

$$\Omega$$

The crammed space inside the barbed wire teems with life. You notice those with limbs missing; 'the amputees', they are called here. You notice the women with babies at breast and small children clinging to a mother's faded sarong. There are children everywhere, impishly shouting the only English they know: 'Okay bye-bye.' Some cluster in a group: little boys naked; little girls with a skirt or knickers, probably not both. Most children's stomachs are swollen with parasites.

This is as I expect it to be; these are the memories I have carried from my visit last year. I balance on a push bike, heading to the Centre for Healing of Heart and Spirit.

My Australian experience has been in community development and social work with traumatised people. I'm on the brink of finding how much I don't know of either.

THAI-CAMBODIA BORDER, 1989

The bike is provided by the Thai Catholic Office of Emergency Relief and Refugees, COERR, pronounced as 'co-err'. The only way forward is to wobble and push through squelchy red-laterite mud and to cross a slippery plank bridge, lurching, narrowly avoiding slithering into water. Here I am in washed-out jeans and crimson cotton tee-shirt mud-splattered already. I hear full-throated laughter, risk my balance and turn my head for a second, then glimpse the man: ancient, wrinkled, skeletal, brown, mouth-wide-open, gummy jaws bare of teeth. He squats on his heels and hoots. Holding the bike still with my right foot planted in the mud I turn and grin back, the two of us linked by laughter. It surely is ridiculous that I can't manage the bike, can't wear proper clothes, am lanky and blotchy pink. I'm glad he can laugh.

In the south of the camp is the Centre for Healing of Heart and Spirit, the Khmer People's Depression Relief, KPDR.

Phaly and Soeun and the team are hard-pressed; happy to see me back, but busy. There is a young woman whose arms are amputated close to her shoulders. As I come through the doorway Phaly notices and covers the stumps with a krama. The woman nods with gratitude as if it is immodest to be seen naked of arms.

I sit to the side, listening to the lilt of the conversations between helper and helped, again smelling the pungent healing herbs, hearing the soft conversations and watching the stroking, the massage, and the gentle soothing. This is the daily rhythm of listening and healing. Sounds merge in gentle rhythm: reassuring the man who fell out of the coconut tree back in Cambodia and can't get his head together any more, massaging saffron-coloured herbs into the body of a woman limp with depression after the birth of her baby, comforting a boy-soldier fresh in from battle. I am hesitant, on edge, wishing I could be useful but not knowing how.

WRITING FOR RAKSMEY

The radio crackles. UNBRO – the United Nations Border Relief Operation – is asking the Centre for a response. In this place without phones, two-way radio requests are public announcements, they echo like commands. KPDR is requested to assist.

This is their problem. A tiny girl like a small, wild animal has made her way inside the UNBRO office and there is no way that the UN staff can restrain her. Someone needs to leave their work and go. Phaly says, 'Joan you can go, you are not busy, this will be good for you to see.' Soeun will come with me; he can deal with the Cambodians, I can talk to the foreigners at UNBRO.

The little girl is called Mom; she looks about five years old. When we find her she is curled up in a ball on the floor with her wrists guarding her face, lashing out with elbows and legs, flailing at anyone who approaches. She is grimy and smells of urine. Her hair is matted and her eyes, when she lets you see them, are wild. I squat down beside her, barely touching her as I stroke her skin. She quietens a little, jolted perhaps by a new experience. I edge closer almost imperceptibly while Soeun talks long and earnestly with the Cambodian UN workers, then closer still, careful to make no sudden movement. Mom turns her head and slides her wrists away from her bloodshot eyes. I hold out my arms. Mom falls into my lap, curls into a damp ball tightly, tightly, and falls asleep. Soeun tells in halting English what he heard in Khmer.

She is known in the camp as the 'crazy girl'. She is eleven years old, though so small. She roams the camp alone and is used for sex. She seems to have fits.

This child is the same size as my beloved little niece, Jess, in Melbourne. I am sitting on the floor with my arms around her, rocking her to and fro.

THAI-CAMBODIA BORDER, 1989

Soeun carries Mom to the American Refugee Committee hospital, a busy bamboo and thatch institution where talented Cambodian medical students are learning from talented medical volunteers. It is clear to me that something should be done to control the fits. A young doctor from Minnesota takes the details; he is interested in the symptoms, eager to consider a diagnosis. He will admit Mom. We should wait; he needs to check with someone more experienced. Eventually he returns, apologetic that he had not known more. He speaks in English, looking at me, avoiding Soeun's gaze.

'Conditions like the fits suffered by this child are not on the list for treatment here.'

I understand. What is permitted under the conditions of the agreement for this camp is limited. The United Nations High Commission for Refugees is not in control; the arrangement is between the Thai government and the United Nations Border Relief Organisation. Our usual professional expectations do not apply.

We both know these facts. We had not considered the implications for this small girl, an illegal immigrant. The American doctor is as new to the camp as I am; we both try to ignore the fact that there are tears in his eyes.

Back at the Centre while Mom sleeps the sleep of exhaustion, Phaly gives me advice. 'Drink tea. You will sweat a lot. Take care not to be dehydrated.'

Ω

I cycle back to the COERR office, a bamboo, thatch and dirt-floor gathering-space, to meet the man who plans to build a Centre for Healing in the northern part of the camp. He waits for me, a painfully thin young man in a spotless white shirt with sleeves turned back to below the elbow and unpressed, freshly washed navy business trousers held up with a brown belt. There are hollows beneath his large, dark eyes. 'My name is Meas Nee.'

I feel too casual and far too smelly. 'Pleased to meet you Mister Nee.'

He has plans. 'There is an old woman and child I want you to see. We will go to her house. Can you ride?'

We cycle along the red-laterite road, then push through mud with no tracks to be seen, wheeling the bikes around puddles, weaving between small bamboo huts.

The house isn't a house, just the remnants of thatch on top of four bamboo poles with a bamboo bench beneath and a little cloth for privacy and shade. The old woman isn't old. She looks eighty to me but is said to be about forty. She is curled on the bench like a foetus. She cannot see any more and can scarcely hear. One eye socket is empty, the other is an immense mass of puss. Her skin, the parchment skin of an old woman, is stretched across her bones.

The neighbours, those who had asked Nee to come, say that the small daughter, the only other member of the family, is away scrounging for food. The husband deserted them long ago; he managed to take the family food-ration book with him.

Nee squats on his heels beside the woman, speaks close to her ear and touches her gently.

The child returns; she nods to Nee's offer to care for them both, and quietly folds up the few possessions. There is no expression on her face. Nee rests his hand lightly on the little girl's shoulder. My hands clutch the handlebars of my bike; my feet are still planted in the mud beside each pedal. I am swamped with pity, immobilised, ashamed of my uselessness, mortified by my own pampered life.

THAI-CAMBODIA BORDER, 1989

A neighbour will transport the woman in a handcart. Nee holds the child's hand. As he pushes his bike through the mud he explains to me in halting English that this eye injury that the mother sustained while scrounging for firewood to sell is not a new injury. Her life has been degenerating for a long time.

'How do you feel about this?' he asks.

What can I say? 'I'm full of sadness for them both, and outraged that this should be. Every person deserves care and dignity.' I don't know Nee yet. Haven't even realised that Meas is his family name and Nee his given name. 'How do you feel?' I ask.

'I have no words' he says.

That night in Ta Phraya I sit, exhausted, on the mattress on the floor, the weight of the day pressing. I write in my journal. 'To walk humbly … perhaps that is all that I can do.'

Ω

Many months later, after we have finished a day of teaching together, Nee tells me a story. 'There was once a village where the people had a hard life. They did not know how they could survive. They ploughed the land the hard way, by hand. They wished they had a buffalo. Then one day they saw a wild buffalo in the jungle. They said they would catch it and tame it.' He looks at me as he speaks. 'They slowly coaxed it to the field. They showed it this new place far from the beautiful green trees it was used to. They hoped that one day it would be useful.'

'Me?' I say. He protests that it was someone else. He protests too much; we are starting to understand each other now. I laugh.

3

INTO THE LIFE OF IT

COERR has provided a single cab utility truck and a new volunteer, Lud Thomassen, a psychiatric nurse from Belgium. We drive together to the camp each morning. The new volunteer is experienced, resourceful and strong; she becomes friend as well as colleague.

The truck has a personality of its own. It is somewhat battered and, unless you know it well, hard to start. On the bumpy tracks the key falls from the ignition while the engine keeps revving and the vehicle continues to move forward. With practice it is possible to steer with the left hand while groping on the floor to find the key and return it to the ignition. It must be found; the engine will only shut down by turning the key to off position. This is no worry. The hardy vehicle that we call 'the Ute' opens new possibilities; small inconveniences are overlooked.

There is a pattern to life and a sense of purpose. My first task each day is to stand with Nee as he completes the planning and preparation for the Centre of Healing in Site 2 North.

Even before a site for the new centre is confirmed he begins to bring potential staff to the COERR office for training. 'You will need to teach us about Western ways of healing the spirit,' he tells me.

Nee remembers and quotes words of advice his father had given before dying as a prisoner of the Khmer Rouge. 'Be a healer, son.

INTO THE LIFE OF IT

When this is over our people will need healers.' With these words in his mind, he has studied every course that Western medical specialists, who regularly volunteer in the camp, offer. He knows about Western treatments for tropical diseases, he can do basic surgery. While studying with the American Refugee Committee he became convinced that Western knowledge and Western drugs could be used side by side with traditional drugs and treatments. During nine years on the border he has seen many traumatised people; his mind is occupied with ways to be a healer.

For my first teaching venture in Site 2 there is a square blackboard tied with string to a bamboo partition in the COERR office. I stand there, chalk in hand. The students are all dressed in their best second-hand donated clothes bought from a pile of assorted garments heaped on a mat at the crossroad. They are sitting in rows with notebooks open, totally attentive. It is the hottest part of the day; they must have sacrificed siesta for this. They are trim and immaculately groomed, the men in long trousers and business shirts, clean and threadbare, the women in well-worn sarongs tight around waist and hips, topped with blouses surely donated by the French. I am hot and sweaty.

Nee introduces me at length in Khmer, then turns to me and says in English, 'Just a few words at a time in English and I will say in Khmer.' I look around at the faces. Twenty or so women and men look back at me expectantly, ballpoint pens ready. 'Thank you. Welcome,' I say. 'Aa kohn. Sohm anjaen,' he echoes. I could easily have said this in Khmer myself; I look at him with a smile and repeat it in Khmer, hoping to relax the class. Nobody laughs. They watch politely.

I take the chalk, grip the swinging blackboard and chalk the letters 'LISTEN'. Nee writes it in Khmer. Everybody writes, and then looks up. 'I have been taught that the first, the most useful thing to do for a person who is really very upset is to listen attentively, to hear what they say.' Nee raises his hand signaling that I should stop. He translates to Khmer; everybody writes then looks to me expectantly. 'I know that you often meet and listen to people who are extremely distressed.' Pause for this to be told in Khmer. 'Nee has told me that it is like being in the bottom of a deep, dark pit.' He nods and interprets. I take the chalk, steady the board, and draw the deep pit with two stick figures at the bottom. Everyone nods, draws, writes and looks up. I draw another stick figure at the top; this one holds a line leading to the one below. 'It is difficult to go down so far in the dark unless there is someone holding a rope for you … to help you get out. It is dangerous to be stuck down there in the darkness.'

I look questioningly at Nee; I have exceeded my quota of words. He looks back and nods. He understands and can take over from here. There is lively interaction. 'Da veng da vo,' he says, then looks sideways to me. I nod, 'To and fro.' When it is time to finish I say to the class, 'I hope one day I will give my opinion and one of you will give your opinion. You will not hesitate to give an opinion that is different from mine. I will be a happy woman and will listen to you just as you listen to me.' Nee says it in Khmer but nobody writes this down.

As we walk from the class Nee tells me that Khmer custom is to listen to the teacher, respect the teacher, memorise what the teacher says. Having a different thought is not Khmer way.

Alone in Ta Phraya I replay the lesson in my mind. Nee talked of a Khmer way to learn, yet when he took control and taught he did not do it that way. Teacher and student looked at experience together and learned together. He was following his instinct, not Khmer way. 'One day soon I will tell him this,' I think.

INTO THE LIFE OF IT

Ω

A small piece of wasteland is available in Site 2 North; it will be the site for the new Centre. We squat down in sparse shade, Nee and I, imagining the buildings that would rise in this barren space. Though it is still rainy season the clouds have not yet massed; the midday heat is searing.

'Of course there will be counsellors,' says Nee. He imagines that counsellors will listen to people's needs and respond to what they hear. He is choosing them from among those coming to the classes in the COERR office: the ones who have the heart for it. 'There will be women and men; some will have a background of Western medicine. They can make partnerships with the hospitals.' We think about it together. Nee wants Western knowledge to be side by side with traditional ways of healing. The counsellors could have training in psychology, human development and community development.

Nee is scratching with a stick in a depression where the ground is still damp: these will be the buildings, these will be the workers. He says 'The traditional healers are good men, keen to start.' These men already know and practice traditional remedies trusted by Cambodians. Since Buddhism is embedded in the culture they should also know when to involve the monks. There are monks in the camp.

The healers and counsellors are the beginning of the team. Until the construction of the buildings is complete Nee will work side by side with them to build the Centre. They will work together as equals, measuring, cutting, tying the bamboo. They will all wear simple working clothes, krama tied round the waist. Building together will help them to share their hopes. They will not be paid with money;

this doesn't happen for him or for anyone. They will each have a few extra kilos of rice as compensation for their families.

Nee has been thinking about a name for this centre. 'Mental Health and Traditional Healing, MHTH,' he says. He likes the sound of it. The buildings will be arranged so that those who come for help can be cared for in the way that would be best for each particular person. He is still drawing with the stick in the mud, adding details as he talks.

After the building is complete each worker will have a specific role. Nee will take his place as director, bring his family to live here and be available for staff who will need to work with inpatients at night as well as during the day.

We walk back to our bikes as the bunched clouds teeter in the afternoon sky. Soft, warm rain splatters down ahead of the deluge. Nee gives no sign of noticing this; his face is tight with thought. 'What do you think about all this?' he asks.

I remind him of his father's words. 'When this is over our people will need healing.'

$$\Omega$$

So much is happening in so short a time. I need to find a quiet place away from the village where I can go regularly to be alone and pray.

It is very early morning as I take the track out of the town to the south, picking my way in the tender light, overtaken and passed by boys herding the family buffalo to the fields. We share the path where the prickly grass is worn down by the heavy hoofs of the animals and the bare feet of the boys.

My own feet are in sandals with their rubber thongs wedged between my toes. I must concentrate on the track as well as looking to the sky where the glow of dawn is seeping in. The track is pocked with heaps of buffalo dung. 'Here I am,' I think to myself. 'Most of my attention is on dodging dung while beauty is all around me.'

The track mounts a slope to a vantage point where the land spread out in the distance is Cambodian land, not Thai land. To my right is the stone wall of a simple Wat. I hear Buddhist chanting, soothing and repetitive. I step off the track in the direction of the Wat; dogs snarl and bark. This brings me to a halt; rabies is endemic here.

As I prepare to abandon my quest a young monk notices and calls the dogs back. He motions to a place for me to sit beside the wall. He sits quietly beside me. The red sun rises.

$$\Omega$$

At COERR headquarters in Bangkok there is a director whose vision fits with Nee's dream. Father Bunlert hopes to strengthen the spirit of the Cambodians in the camp, to free them to be leaders each in their own way. He sees potential for good in everyone he meets and will do whatever he can for this to develop. He was a young leader in times of struggle in Thailand; he wants to support, not to control. He believes that the Centre Nee dreams about can become a reality. 'Nee is a good man,' he tells me. 'Work with him.'

Nee is preoccupied with calculating and ordering materials for the building, with forging relationships among potential team members, with connecting to all who must authorise the land for the new venture. UNBRO will deliver bamboo to the site: high centre poles for each main area, sturdy corner poles, lighter bamboo for the framework, bamboo lattice for windows, and thatch for roofing. While sharing his enthusiasm I notice he is becoming even thinner.

Lud is alarmed and clinical. 'If he is losing weight so fast he should take the test for TB; he is a medic. He must know that rapid weight loss requires a diagnosis. He will listen to you; talk to him about it.'

'He's a competent adult. I don't push him to talk about what he doesn't want to talk about.'

'You have to. He will listen to you.'

After a routine meeting with Nee I enquire about his wife Monee, as I know that she is pregnant. I hesitate then enquire about his own health, saying that friends worry that he may have TB.

Nee looks at me for a few moments without comment. His medical knowledge is far in advance of mine; I have crossed a line that I immediately regret crossing. 'It isn't TB.' He speaks kindly as if giving a lesson to a group of new medics: not arrogant but informative. He reminds me that the UNBRO ration is exactly enough to sustain life. It is called humane deterrence; they don't want to attract people from inside Cambodia to come to the border just because they are hungry. They try to balance enough protein, enough carbohydrate to sustain life. No more. A pregnant woman needs more for herself and for the baby. 'This is our baby. I can do with less. Monee needs more.'

Next morning Lud and I begin to smuggle eggs into the camp. Under the seat of the Ute, below the broken springs but above the floor is a space the right size for a small packet of fresh eggs. The young Thai guards search the Ute day after day without uncovering anything amiss, or at least not mentioning it if they do notice. Challenging Lud may need more courage than they can muster. Our egg delivery becomes part of our routine.

Though the eggs are delivered Nee remains thin and gaunt.

INTO THE LIFE OF IT

Ω

On an ordinary morning as I arrive from Ta Phraya ready to start work, Nee is waiting for me with more urgency than usual. 'Come to my house. Come now.' I cycle after him, catching his excitement, guessing. Resting my bike against the wall of his home of bamboo and blue plastic sheeting, I stoop through the doorway and adjust to the dim light inside.

It is a small room with the bamboo bench-bed filling much of the space. Monee is resting there dressed in fresh sarong fastened under her arm pits, her shoulders bare, her face pale and her dark hair loose. Her baby, born in the night, is a boy, perfectly formed. He lies on his stomach across his mother's knees. She strokes his bare back with her right hand while her left cups his head. She smiles briefly then looks down again, absorbed in the tiny boy.

Monee's mother sits beside her, her task well done. She has delivered the baby and cleansed him. She has burned the sarong her daughter wore during the birth. She has massaged the new mother with saffron coloured herbs and lit the small charcoal fire under the bed bench. This small space smells of smoke and herbs. Monee's bare shoulders and face glisten with sweat. All is according to tradition.

Monee is strikingly beautiful: full lips, high cheekbones, skin smooth and honey tan. Her face is rounded in the manner of classic Khmer attractiveness. Her husband crosses the room and stands close to her: gaunt, darker, and with circles under his eyes. Their daughter Srey Leak stands to the side, huge eyes thoughtful, lips pressed tightly together. Her limbs are rounded; she is a normal little three-year-old here in this camp of skinny children. Her father's arm rests lightly around her, protective. With two hands she grips a blue mug with 'Angkor Wat' stencilled in white on its side. Her short dark hair is cut in a fringe, glossy and abundant.

The newborn baby brother is to be called Raksmey. He is healthy, so is his mother. His father is more than content.

I become part of the joy, congratulating everyone, speaking in faltering Khmer to the shy Monee and to her mother.

4

CROSSFIRE

As soon as the rains stop, as soon as the mud bakes hard, as soon as tanks can move across the land, battles rage once more in Cambodia.

In Ta Phraya just before dawn each morning a squad of Thai men in uniform pounds down the street in a rhythmic synchronised jog, huffing in unison, precise in columns and lines. Bemused, I watch through my window. Thai troops are on alert. Covered army trucks stop on the roadside close to my house in the middle of the night. Male voices wake me, negotiating to buy something from a shopkeeper nearby, but I cannot distinguish the language or see what is sold. I'm careful not to be noticed as I watch.

Inexorably the frontline of battle draws closer to the camp and to Ta Phraya. We hear shelling day and night. Singapore sends two covert arms shipments, including anti-tank weapons. These weapons find their way into Khmer Rouge hands. The Khmer Rouge under Ta Kok overrun Anlong Veng, close to the Thai border. Government forces from Phnom Penh bombard the Khmer Rouge territory.

When the sound of battle is too close to be ignored rumours sweep through the camp. Cambodians who have begun to trust me tell me that Khmer Peoples' National Liberation Front leaders, who hold power in camp administration, may deliberately ensure that women and children and the elderly are not evacuated to a place further from the shelling, as civilian casualties could draw international attention to this conflict. If this happens the cost in human suffering will be appalling. Everybody in the camp is fearful. Most have already experienced the terror of shells dropping around them and seen loved ones die.

It is Wednesday morning. After a week of tension the danger to Site 2 is now immediate. Situation One, the first I have experienced, is declared. It is the routine warning that the threat is real. Everybody knows.

UNBRO has a protocol to protect the lives of a few score foreign workers but not the lives of scores of thousands of refugees. As a foreigner I am required to carry a two-way field radio 'at all times' during this crisis, and to await instructions. In mid-morning Situation Two is declared; I must return immediately to the Centre for Healing and wait there. I wait. The next call could be a return to Situation One or could be either Situation Three or Four.

My Cambodian friends and colleagues do not carry field radios to instruct them; since they have lived through this many times they show me what to do. If Situation Four is suddenly called I must do what they have often done: when shells begin to fall, lie face down in a ditch or in the lowest place available, shield face, head and vital organs from flying shrapnel, protect myself if I can.

At lunchtime Situation Three is called. Foreigners must evacuate in a convoy of motor vehicles. No foreigner is permitted to stay in danger; no Cambodian is permitted to leave. I follow the radio instruction to 'proceed out of the camp in an orderly manner' and taste the bitter bile of claiming privilege and leaving others defenceless. My name must be checked off from the UNBRO list.

Back in Ta Phraya I listen to the shelling and write letters to send as faxes to people of influence in Australia, beginning with Bob Hawke, the Prime Minister:

> I wonder if I can convey the feeling of the volunteers as we are driven to safety in air-conditioned vehicles and carefully checked from a list held by the United Nations Border Relief Operation: well protected while 170,000 people are still behind the fences of that shelled area and are kept there by armed guards. Half of the refugees are children, of the rest most are women. I don't think I can convey to you what it is like to watch their faces as we drive out … people gather against the barbed wire fence furthest from the shelling. But nobody cuts the wires! They wait, they hope, for the military guards to give permission to evacuate.

There is no evacuation. The sound of war is unrelenting. The boy-conscripts I have seen carried off in the Khmer People's National Liberation Front's open trucks are surely in the thick of the suffering and dying.

Ta Phraya is safe even when the frontline is said to be less than three kilometres away. This Thai community is not a target. The sound of 'shelling-out' can be distinguished from 'shelling-in', Phaly has told me. 'Shelling-out starts with a sound like a sarong ripping.' I follow the sound of the battle. When Phnom Penh government troops shell in, the Thai troops and the KPNLF troops shell out. Darkness comes. On the horizon where shells are falling the sky flickers with light.

I am on my knees in every way: trying to pray, unable to sleep, wrestling with God. I write letters with little sensitivity to the friends who would receive them, write to distract myself and to let the sheltered world 'out there' know of this outrage.

Ω

Site 2 remains closed to the barang day after day, for as long as the immediate danger lasts. Day and night the dull thud of shelling is unyielding. I realise that war is work for those who man the guns. The Khmer word for work is in my mind. Tveu kah. This is the sound. Tveu kah. Tveu kah. The rhythm of the word is the rhythm of the thudding. This is day and night work, to destroy.

I am thinking of the Khmer word for dead. It sounds like slah!p. It throbs.

> Slah!p.
> The mother of the innocent
> weeping, weeping now,
> the curtain of her life
> is ripped in sobs
> convulsive shuddering
> of frail pale body
> spending with abandon
> all last strength on grief.
>
> slah!p.
> Grief for the children who
> still must live
> and watch her now
> with wondering eyes.
>
> slah!p. slah!p. slah!p. slah!p. slah!p.
> Like Rachel weeping for her children

she cannot be comforted
because they are no more.

Ω

I write to Australia of things too obscene to be written, needing the world to know what I have seen.

> This week there was a father with the sole care of a precious baby daughter. He sold everything he had for tinned milk to keep the baby alive. He even sold his trousers, but the baby died. He stood in line in his underpants at the makeshift crematorium, an open fire. He placed the little corpse wrapped in his hand-woven krama, a cotton scarf, onto the grill. We stood with him; the best we had been able to do for him was to make his wait in line shorter; we heard the crackling sound and smelt burning flesh.

Ω

The shelling has stopped, the danger has passed, we have permission to return to the camp. The mood of the Cambodians here has changed from fear to mourning. The monks are moving from house to house chanting the traditional chants for the dead. A great many KPNLF soldiers, including many conscripts new and untrained on the battlefield, have died. It seems that the chanting will never stop: it is so loud, so incessant, that conversation is impossible.

Phaly asks me to sit with a young soldier, Keing, who has been brought to the Centre crazed with anguish. Keing sits on a piece of blue plastic in a darkened corner where a single thread of light comes through a slit in the bamboo wall. His eyelids close across empty sockets. Everything is darkness for him. He is wearing a check flannelette shirt unbuttoned, and underpants. His head is bowed, his shoulders hunched. His bare right leg is flat on the ground in lotus position. His left knee is raised to his chest; he hugs his arms around it so that one hand grasps his ankle. I notice that his fingers are long and tapered, musician's hands, perhaps, in a different life.

I hear his story. Keing's father and mother, brother and sisters died in Khmer Rouge times. He honoured his army commander in place of the father he had lost. He did not hesitate when the commander asked him to crawl ahead through a field. A landmine exploded, his limbs were intact but his face and eyes bore the brunt of the flying fragments. In the battlefield tent-clinic the medics removed his eyes. Day after day he waits for the commander. The commander does not come.

Tears flow down Keing's face from the tear ducts at the edge of his empty eye sockets, he believes that his eyes could have been saved. After many weeks he will feel my face and lips and eyes.

This time I am more sensitive in what I write back to Australia:

> Keing, a young man just recently blinded in the war, has become a friend. In his grief he was particularly alone as he has no family members alive 'after Pol Pot.' He is strong, handsome, gentle and intelligent but his eye sockets are hollow and empty. One by one I have met his friends and begun to know their capacity to help Keing and to help me … They are loving, challenging, open about their own feelings of anguish as tears stream from Keing's empty eyes.

In truth it is anguish for anybody to be close to Keing. We look for some way to soften his terrible grief. He is alert to the sound of music. I bring a cassette player and many batteries from Ta Phraya. He listens.

Ω

When the shelling around the border ceases, a small village just inside Cambodia is flattened by an attack from the Phnom Penh troops. It is not the usual attack. It is a hail of heavy rockets coming from a Russian multiple-missile launcher, many kilometres distant. Missiles follow each other second by second. This deluge makes a distinctive screaming sound. The weapon is not precisely accurate over the distance. It is designed to terrify the neighbourhood. Ammunition of such sophistication has not been heard in these parts before. Forty people are confirmed dead, though many more are not accounted for.

Two hundred surviving villagers flee to Site 2 for refuge. They are, of course, illegal immigrants here. They are stripped of all their possessions as the bribe for 'permission to cross' and are provided with a little rice and water as they huddle miserably in the same pagoda where monks chant day and night lamenting the dead soldiers.

One night a recently married soldier, traumatised by what he has seen and perhaps by what he has done, comes home to the camp, puts his two arms around his wife and pulls the pin on a hand grenade. They both die instantly.

Nee calls me aside. 'This is hard for you,' he says. 'We have been here for nine years already. You get used to it.'

Ω

In Ta Phraya on a hot afternoon I trudge between the rows of dry stubble left behind from newly cut rice. The sun, though still strong, is lowering. Sunlight shimmers; it bounces in a heat haze.

I walk alone with my thoughts digging deeper into a groove of dilemmas. This is not the straightforward refugee camp that I imagined it to be.

My feet in rubber thongs sink in the dust; they drag with chaff between toes. Though I long for a breeze, just the slightest movement of air, I keep slogging and sweating. I sweat over a question. I need to be alone to think.

The Thai authorities see Site 2 as a detention camp for illegal immigrants. They are glad to have this buffer zone while the Vietnamese armies are still in Cambodia. Vietnam and Thailand harbour traditional enmities. Vietnam is supported by the USSR and Thailand by the USA.

The Cambodian warring faction controlling the camp, the Khmer Peoples' National Liberation Front, sees it as a strategic military base where civilian refugees attract foreign aid and provide a pool of conscripts for their army.

And me? What does my presence do? Give credibility to a ruthless armed faction? I feel the sweat trickling down my body plastering clothes to skin. Where is truth?

The orb of sun grows big and orange as it lowers in the sky. The harvesters in a distant field are finishing for the day. One comes in my direction: Bob, a friend with chaff and dust clinging to him. 'Will you go or will you stay?'

The sun slips from sight. Buffalos track back to the village with the buffalo-boys calling to urge them home. There comes a breeze, not strong, just enough to halt my trudging.

'Will you go or will you stay?' This is the quandary. The crocodile in the water or the tiger on the shore. To stay would add another gram of legitimacy to the warring faction, the Khmer People's National

Liberation Front, holding the refugees captive. To go would mean walking away from refugee friends who work to make this place more bearable for others. They are trapped here but they inspire me. They would say, 'Of course you should stay.'

Darkness closes in. The smell of buffalo dung is strong now; it is earthy. I reach for the one edge of a truth that I can hold. It is a simple thing to stay where goodness manages to flourish, even if I know there is corruption all around.

The lights of the village guide me back through the darkness. As I make my way to the small timber house to write, all the dogs of the neighbourhood bark.

I stay. Right or wrong, I stay.

$$\Omega$$

I can never get used to being the one to evacuate from the camp while others are left in danger. After being driven to safety time and again I begin to wonder whether it would be noticed if I simply ignored the radio message.

Situation 3 is called. Nee and Tolla and Bora come to the place where I am teaching. I can hear the horn of the Ute blaring. Nee is driving, swaggeringly doing wheelies on the dusty ground, tooting the horn. I have taught him to drive.

Tolla and Bora are standing at the back, clowning, each trying to shout louder than the other.

'Have to save the barang, she is very precious.'

'Slow down, slow down, she can jump on board if you drive slowly.'

'Get her out of here'.

5

TA PHRAYA

I live in the Thai village of Ta Phraya, twenty kilometres or so from Site 2. It is as close to the camp as foreigners are permitted to live. For some of us expats Ta Phraya is a haven, though many choose to live in Aranyaprathet, a larger town further from Site 2.

Rice fields surround the village. The farmers who live in small houses on stilts in the simple streets of unpaved roads shelter their animals under the house at night then bring the buffalo to their fields by day. I rent a small, raw-timber Thai house and revel in the sound of geckos, the smell of rain on rice fields and vistas of intense wet-season green.

My neighbours awaken at the first crowing of a rooster: already the Buddhist monks walk silently through the town, begging bowls held before them, saffron robes brilliant against weathered houses and shuttered shops.

As soon as the light is strong enough the town is ready for the busyness of the day. The metal door of a roofed area known as the 'Barang Shop' rolls up and goods that the barang might want to buy are on display: long-life milk, coffee, mosquito coils, prickly heat powder, tea bags, very rarely, butter, very, very rarely, bread; overseas air letters, toilet paper. Toilet paper is popular with better-off Thai customers too, displayed in a hand-carved timber holder in the middle of the meal table it is used as serviettes. The Barang Shop is the place for the expats to meet, to organise the day before the early morning journey to the camp, or to buy a cool drink in the evening before going home.

$$\Omega$$

I welcome any chance of evening mass. Especially during the most hazardous times, many volunteers and workers of any faith or no faith gather in a house rented by priests of the Jesuit Refugee Service. There is a small room with a low table for an altar, a simple setting for this ritual. The book of scripture is open. We sit around the table on cushions on the floor silently recalling the day that has been. Together we listen to the scripture; in the Eucharist we remember the death and resurrection of Jesus. As the orange glow of tropical sunset dims, the light of a candle already flickering on the table seamlessly replaces it.

'Jesus said, "Heal the broken-hearted, set the prisoners free".' It is simple and clear. We have spent our day with the heartbroken; those with no choices. There is no dogma, no rhetoric. Familiar words break the silence after a day of struggling with longings and doubts. There is one sure thing: Jesus' choice was to take the side of the most oppressed, to join with them.

$$\Omega$$

Night-life in downtown Ta Phraya is simple: a cool dipper-shower, fresh light clothes, a good slathering of mosquito repellent and a meal with friends.

Near the main street is a popular roadside wok where noodle dishes and rice dishes are stir-fried to order. On request they can be topped with a fried egg or two. Here there are tin tables and tin stools. Around the corner is a small cafe known as the 'Chicken Curry' in honor of its signature meal. Customers sit on plastic chairs and eat at plastic tables. Out of town, too far to walk, is the one we call the Golden Buffalo. Here the guests sit on chairs of jungle timber, at carved tables hand crafted and polished. The Golden Buffalo serves what the menu describes as steak.

My friends favour the roadside wok. We dine under the stars when there is need to talk about the happenings of the day. The meal begins with cool drinks: iced lime juice with sugar and salt in a ratio measured to counteract dehydration, then beer, coke or soda water. Individual orders are tossed in the wok. Hot fat spits, the flames flare. Often there is laughter; if the day has been weighted with tragedy there is grief. We remember our friends in the camp who cannot share the support that we offer to each other.

On one such night we begin to plan for a session of training in Ta Phraya. We write a proposal for the Cambodians of the Centre for Healing and some of their colleagues to be permitted to leave the camp for 'study'. The 'study' would involve a small group of border Khmer coming to Ta Phraya for a weekend. This could be repeated at different times for different groups. The plan is submitted and astoundingly it is approved.

$$\Omega$$

TA PHRAYA

Six Cambodians, four men and two women, competent and creative leaders, refugees though called illegal immigrants, are given permission to study outside of the camp for a few days.

They show their passes to the Thai guards then leave Site 2 in the back of the COERR Ute. Once outside the barbed wire they are in a countryside that is impoverished but free. Rice fields, coconut palms, pigs, chickens, small clusters of Thai houses, Thai mothers-fathers-children piled together on family motorbikes.

In the back of the Ute Thavy, Phaly, Soeun, Sok Thim and Nee note each detail. Their children in the camp have never seen such sights, have never even smelled the growing rice. Their talk starts with 'If only …', and 'I wish …'

Bora, the youngest, the one not yet married, does not join this talk. He wants to tell me what he remembers, scrunching his face as he begins. He was the only member of his family to survive the Khmer Rouge times, as far as he knows. He recalls sitting on an ox cart travelling north, feeling that he was alone in the world, wanting to get far away from the place of his suffering. He was still very young at this time.

I watch him as he speaks. His face, always mobile, has lost its playful expression and has collapsed into furrows, his shoulders are hunched. As we sit crammed together in the back of the Ute I can picture him as a boy, legs dangling over the edge of the cart. He tells me that after they had all travelled for a long time he began to notice that the man beside him, an 'older man' of about forty years, was quietly sobbing.

I wonder whether this was uncomfortable for a child or whether perhaps it was companionable to be with an older stranger who suffered too. The memory remains with him, both the silent grief and the words that were eventually spoken, 'Boy, what is your name?' He repeats these words, they are still important to him. 'Boy, what is your name?'

In the man's home village in Battambang Province the man and the boy climbed down from the cart together. The man's small daughter was still alive; nobody else in the family had survived. Bora tells me that he stayed with them for a time then seized another opportunity to go ahead through the minefields to the border. We sit together in silent thought for the rest of the journey.

On the main street of Ta Phraya we walk past the dusty shops, past the bus stops, to the other end of town. There is no longer any thought of a formal workshop. This rapid immersion into ordinary life, and the chance to talk about it, is more than enough.

Soeun, a city man educated in Phnom Penh, can name the make of each car and truck parked at the side of the road. Before the Khmer Rouge he had an important role in a petrol company. He has not forgotten.

Phaly pauses at the entrance of the 'Beauty Shop', intrigued by the buzz of Thai voices, women's gossip. Local women sit around waiting to have their hair washed, cut, curled and dyed and their fingernails and toenails painted. Posters around the plywood walls depict in vivid colour the treatments that are on offer. There is a bamboo bench where the one being shampooed lies on her back gazing at the sagging, rain-stained cardboard ceiling, her head suspended over a plastic dish. Expert hands massage her temples and scalp and rinse off the lavender-scented suds with dipper after dipper of water. Much more water than a whole family in Site 2 would have for a day. Phaly understands massage. She understands attractiveness and the routines to achieve it. She carries her beauty consciously, her shoulder length curly hair, her rounded features and ready smile. 'Dohj knia sroh!k Khmai,' she says with satisfaction. It is just like Cambodia.

The early-morning Thai market bustles with life, purposeful, ordinary and carefree. Our Cambodian friends, though they are natural leaders among their people in the camp, stand awkwardly. Beams of light filter from high in the roof: sunlight falls upon fruit, vegetables, eggs, rice, poultry, meat and fish. Such abundance, such over-abundance, of food. Usable fruit and vegetable scraps are trodden under foot, even rice grains are spilled a little. Vendors shout their wares, buyers bargain. I wonder whether our friends have noticed the small tins of fish intended as food for the needy but finding their way to the Ta Phraya market: the Japanese flag on the label, the English lettering, 'Gift from Japan'.

Hens squawk in bamboo cages, fish swim in buckets. I remember that these Cambodians are all hungry. The smell of the food stalls around the perimeter of the market space pulls like a magnet. They choose noodle soup and rice soup rich with chicken or pork, fragrant with spices, sold in transparent plastic bags, held carefully like intravenous drips in a hospital. We go home. Sheltered inside the house they are ready to eat their fill. There is no restriction.

Sitting on a straw mat spread on the floor they eat seriously without words until the food is finished. In the privacy of this place where doors can close, where walls are strong, where conversations cannot be overheard, they tell stories never told, give opinions never uttered, in the camp. Here there is an easy stream of talk.

Nee looks around the room. 'In the camp I feel as if I am living under the edge of the roof of someone else's house.' He talks of the checkpoint between the north and the south of the camp where, on Sunday, when there are usually no barang to observe what is happening, Thai guards require the Cambodians to crouch down in order to pass through. The guards look for small excuses to beat them with rods. One Cambodian has the cuff of his shirt turned up unevenly, another has not crouched down low enough, soon enough. They are hauled out of the line to be beaten. Nee tells of dignity being drained away, of women and men being driven to fearfulness and then ridiculed for letting those feelings show.

Sitting at ease – as people do in the house of a friend, comfortable in this room with cushions on the floor, curtains at the windows, and pictures on the walls – they start to tell stories of Khmer Rouge times.

As the conversation begins they seem to be saying things that they want the barang to know. They tell of 'Pol Pot days', of working in the fields from early morning until late night, desperate with hunger and numb with fear, numb to the point of following orders with blind obedience. They talk of staying just barely alive on a diet of watery rice soup, obsessed with getting something into their stomachs, of chewing grass in desperation until their stool looked like the stool of animals.

Sok Thim says that their captors thought of them as animals. Thavy says that they knew they must obey everything without thought in order to stay alive. There was no decision that they were free to make. Nee talks of his night-blindness; it was the result of malnutrition. If the Khmer Rouge noticed it he would have been killed like a useless animal. Those who could no longer work were battered to death. When the mobile youth team was led out to work in the darkness before dawn and when they returned from work at night Nee could not see at all. His friend held a stick for him to grasp; he was led as one would lead a dog. There was no dignity left.

The guests rest in the heat of the day and are invited to take a dipper shower with abundant water. They emerge through the back door of the house one by one fresh and relaxed, the men with kramas wrapped around them from waist to knees, Phaly and Thavy with hair shampooed and conditioned, faces creamed, sarongs tied neatly from under their arm pits. They have washed their clothes and draped them over trees to dry in the sunshine.

Phaly says, 'During Khmer Rouge times I would try to spread a krama on the ground, place the family's dish of watery soup on it and a wild flower beside it.' I can well believe it. Even here, dressed only in a sarong, she is gracious and elegant.

$$\Omega$$

Soeun, the first man from the shower, pours cool drinks, adds some chips of ice from the ice bin and joins me outside in the shade. He is ready to talk politics and guesses I am interested to learn. We are about the same age. But our lives, lived parallel in time, have been vastly different. 'Soeun, I'm wondering about when you first came to the border,' I say.

He looks thoughtfully down at his drink, clinks the ice in the glass and hesitates. His hair is still plastered wet against his head from the shower; he is a man on holiday, watching the hens squawking and scratching in the yard. He points to a huge tree across the way, recognising. 'That is a soup tree,' he says, then settles down to tell what he knows.

The first refugees fled to the border of Thailand at the same time as the Vietnamese 'liberating army' from the south moved north in their offensive against the Khmer Rouge. From the beginning those who fled ahead of the fighting were a mixed group clustered at first on the Cambodian side of the border, later on the Thai side.

I notice Soeun's soft-spoken poise. He is explaining this in his second or probably third language. I imagine the contribution he would make if he lived in a place where his leadership could flourish. We are enjoying the chance of being free to talk. It is as though we have all met socially for the first time.

He tells me that among the early ones to reach the border were Khmer Rouge who simply wanted to get away from the Vietnamese army. Some of the early-comers were given refuge in the USA. The possibility of refuge in a third country lasted only for a very brief time; after that, those who crossed the border in this area were called 'illegal immigrants'. Disciplined Khmer Rouge soldiers took to the jungle-clad mountains, especially around Palin. They bided their time and mounted skirmishes against the Vietnamese army.

We refill our glasses and offer drinks and ice to the others relaxing in the shade.

Followers of Prince Sihanouk clung to the hope that the royal kingdom could be established again. Many made their way to the border to set up royalist encampments. Their leaders were also ready to mount resistance to the Vietnamese. They chose a French acronym and formed the FUNCINPEC army.

'What about you, Soeun?' I ask.

Cool and at ease, Soeun gestures with his hands, rattling the ice in his glass, shaping my understanding. Many educated Cambodians, Phaly and himself among them, wanted to work for a different Cambodia. They knew of democracy and they feared communism of any kind. They also clustered close to the Thai Border. From their encampments, and from those who joined with them, resistance leaders were trained. They developed the KPNLF, Khmer People's National Liberation Front.

The three younger men have come from the house slick with shower water. They squat on their heels in the shade, within hearing of Soeun. His experience is different from theirs. They listen.

They all know that KPNLF, FUNCINPEC and the Khmer Rouge, three very different factions, are supported by the USA and other Western nations. I know that this ill-matched group is recognised by the United Nations as 'Democratic Kampuchea'; it occupies the seat for Cambodia at the UN headquarters in New York. 'This worries me Soeun,' I say. He nods and tells me that refugees who stumble into the camp of one of these factions are automatically counted as supporting the faction that controls the camp.

We all know that the luckiest refugees, or those able to pay competent guides, stumble across the border adjacent to the only UNHCR camp, Khao I Dang. This camp is never attacked by any of the warring factions. At Khao I Dang you can be safe and there could be a chance to be settled in a third country if you are too afraid to return to Cambodia.

$$\Omega$$

Late in the afternoon, when Ta Phraya begins to cool, the guests decide to walk along the south track to a hill outside the village. There will be a view across into Cambodia. They have all lost their awkwardness; they are striding confidently between the rice fields, first smiling and then laughing.

They stand on the rise, Cambodia spread in front of them. The laughter stops. There is silence.

Sok Thim speaks first. 'The spirit of our people has survived but it has become very low. Too much oppression for too long. I remember seeing an old woman of our people kneeling right down in the dust in front of a barang, begging for help. She was shaking all over. That night I could see her in my mind still. Tears came to my eyes. We lack everything that people need. We want to build our country; we need to build the spirit of the people first.'

They are bunched together now, looking at their country. Nee says, 'I ask myself why I feel this humiliation even more than in Khmer Rouge times. I think that I am emerging from numbness and beginning to feel.'

$$\Omega$$

It is later in the same week. I cycle through the camp, carrying a field radio as I am required to do. I hear a message: staff at the COERR hospital need urgent backup because a crazy man is hacking down the bamboo walls of the hospital with an axe. When I arrive Soeun is crouched in the dirt beside the agitated patient, stroking him gently, speaking softly, and pouring soothing water over him as the monks do. Nee is beside him. The axe is out of sight of the patient, behind Nee's back.

6

HEALING

MHTH, the centre for Mental Health and Traditional Healing, begins to receive patients as soon as the building tools are laid down. It is as though a stream of needy people have come from nowhere.

Men, women and children walk in groups along the red-laterite road in front of the bamboo hospital of Médecins Sans Frontières, turn left into a smaller, rougher road, then turn left again, creating a pathway as they walk across to the new Mental Health and Traditional Healing buildings.

Those who have come for traditional remedies squat patiently on their heels, waiting their turn. Women with babes in arms look for shade or use a krama to shield the sun and keep the baby cool. The air is filled with the smoke and the fragrance of herbs, aromatic bark and leaves. The healers are calm, weather-beaten men. They have an air of pride. What they do here is what they know best. The patients are content to wait.

Further up the track a counselling class is serious about learning ways of restraining a violent patient. They practise on each other, amazed that this can be done without hurting the patient. A barang from UNBRO, a large and strong man, calls to enquire about the official opening of the centre. He is sceptical about any attempt at non-violent restraint. While he is still explaining his reasons for scepticism the counsellors surprise him, lifting him from his feet. He struggles but is held firmly and effectively, horizontal above the ground. The class erupts into laughter. He laughs too.

$$\Omega$$

The day to celebrate the opening of MHTH is blue and clear. The rainy season is over, the early dry season sparkles with freshness, the bamboo buildings are decked with coloured paper chains. From Bangkok, from Aranyaprathet, from throughout the camp, invited guests come to the new MHTH to celebrate the opening with chanting of saffron robed monks, with food and with speeches. Nee's speech in Khmer is easy and fluent. His speech in English is well practised. He invites the guests to look at the vegetable garden, the traditional healing buildings, the fish pond, the counselling buildings, the new – he hesitates here – 'chicken, no not chicken, kitchen'. The guests applaud; MHTH is launched.

Guests are served a hot meal from large pots of rice and soup that simmer over open fires behind the new buildings. COERR has provided funds for this. Even as the guests celebrate, the counsellors are quietly working among the patients in the bamboo ward. The ceremony is simply another event during a busy week.

$$\Omega$$

I watch the MHTH team of women and men arrive one by one to start the work each day. We greet as friends and share fragments of news before the work begins.

HEALING

'Sok sahbahy!' Greetings to Thavy, a counsellor, as she comes up the track on the back of her husband's pushbike. Thavy is a short, sturdy, motherly woman, one with typical Cambodian features: large eyes, soft dark curls and dusky skin. She grins as she steadies her feet on the ground. 'Ot bpanyhah,' she says. No problems. I smile back to her; it is a relief to us all that there are no problems. Thavy, probably near the end of her child-bearing years, is pregnant. She is adamant that she will not leave her work at MHTH until she goes into labour. 'Why should I?' she asks. 'What else would I do?'

Thavy works with women who need to protect themselves from abuse. MHTH has gathered together a group of eleven vulnerable women to support each other. Where bamboo and blue plastic shelters are crammed together so that no conversation is private, where anger is already out of control by the time neighbours become aware of it, these women have been helped to devise a plan.

The woman who is first to hear the start of violence will beat on her cooking pot. Each other woman, as she hears the beating of a cooking pot, will find a cooking pot and beat it. They will run to the place of the violence, beating and beating at their cooking pots. The violent man will lose face in front of ten or eleven women standing together, making a great noise.

Thavy explains to me that there is no effective law to protect a woman. For a woman to approach the justice committee or, even more daringly, to seek a divorce, requires extraordinary courage. Until recently a woman was not permitted to file for divorce. Only the man could do that. It was his right. Even now the members of the justice committee are all men; they have not changed in attitude that the wife is the property of her husband. Thavy says, 'It is still the woman who has to suffer.'

WRITING FOR RAKSMEY

Ω

A wildly agitated man is brought in to the centre. The first thought is that he is psychotic. This patient needs to be restrained. Nee decides to take the night watch; it would be unsafe to leave a patient in this condition with someone less experienced. He observes the agitation, tries to calm the man but cannot quell the paranoia. He sits beside him through the night charting an abnormally high fever, restraining him with a silk krama, speaking soothingly. By morning he knows that this is not a matter for traditional medicine or counselling. It is a parasite attacking the man's brain. This is cerebral malaria. His patient is probably a soldier who has been brought in from the mosquito-ridden jungle. The man's condition is critical but there is treatment for cerebral malaria. The patient has a chance to survive.

At the end of the day, when all that can be done by the combined effort of the team has been done, there is, as usual, a 'goodbye', laced with laughter. Someone says 'I have never laughed so much in all my life.' At the centre of it is Thavy, with Tolla; they seem to always manage this ending of the day, a village woman clowning with a city man.

7

BIRTH

Theary is a talented Cambodian refugee midwife, so Nee tells me. He would like to introduce me to her as his vision and hers are similar. Theary's obstetric ward at Médecins Sans Frontières is no more than two-hundred metres from MHTH.

I'm surprised to be greeted at the entrance of the ward by a slim young woman with dark, curling hair tucked back behind her ears. She is welcoming though she seems to be rather shy. This is not my image of a nurse responsible for staff and patients in a busy maternity ward serving one third of the population of this camp. Theary speaks English well.

Our first visit is formal. She shows us the labour ward with a bamboo partition for privacy and a bamboo bench for the delivery. There is no electricity or running water but Theary is ready with an improvised humidicrib, a nest made of the silver bladders from the inside of the barangs' empty wine casks. They can be filled with hot water. The little labour ward has a neatly lettered sign in Khmer: No Spitting in Here Please.

Theary's team is having a meal break in the late morning. I can hear lunch-room chatter and laughter. The nurses are sharing food they have cooked and brought from home. Since they are all refugees the language of this ward is Khmer; observations and notes are written in their first language. All have equal chance to develop professionally.

Theary moves among the patients on the ward, some in the last stages of pregnancy, some with a babe in arms. She is reassuring and friendly as she hears their stories and checks their charts.

Next time I return without Nee and bring food to share so that I can be part of the easy chatter in the bamboo-partitioned staff area. The lunch-room chatter becomes more serious; the mid-wives are taking the opportunity to tell me that women in this camp suffer in many ways, not only because of their detention. They describe what they have been seeing: women beaten by their husbands, women who have been raped, women who are destitute, 'taxi girls' who sleep with men for money and are vulnerable to STDs. They say that the families of soldiers are the poorest in the camp; this poverty leads to many problems including medical ones.

Often new parents in the care of this midwifery team choose to honour traditional rituals of birth: the father buries the placenta at the threshold of the family's shelter or at a place where people gather, the mother is massaged with the traditional herbs, the traditional fire is lit under her bamboo bench.

Theary can ensure that Western knowledge is available and is used; the potential for partnership with MHTH is obvious.

I'm keen to learn from the way that the ward is set up. 'How did you do it?' I ask. She smiles and the serious professional role slips for a minute. 'Mary Dunbar encouraged me.' I am making a mental note to find this Mary and talk to her. Mary is no longer in the ward now that Theary is leading; this is the way I would want to do it.

$$\Omega$$

BIRTH

One afternoon, after the work of the day has finished, Thavy feels strong contractions and knows that labour has definitely begun. This is not her first child. On the way to the border, in danger and destitution, the first two children of the family, both little girls, died of hunger. Though Thavy now has three young boys, she and her husband still mourn their daughters. Thavy admires Theary and knows her skills; she has arranged to go to the Médecins Sans Frontières hospital for this delivery. We wait for news.

Thavy gives birth to a baby daughter. Joy spreads fast. Soon after the birth Thavy and the precious child are 'dinked' home on the back of the proud father's pushbike. The child is called Sopheak. She is dressed in pink and her brothers lean over her, awed, as she is held to her mother's breast. We crowd into the tiny hut to admire Sopheak. Thavy tells us all that the name means 'the straight, true path'.

Thavy is stroking Sopheak's small forehead, smoothing the silky skin with her thumb. When she cradles the tiny bundle of baby tenderly in the crook of her arm the father and all three brothers are never far away. Sopheak is three days old when an Australian Broadcasting Corporation journalist and a cameraman find their way to Site 2 and Thavy, still holding little Sopheak close to her, is ready to talk to them about the straight, true path that women in this place are challenged to take.

She speaks into the microphone of the rule of divorce: the first child of the union and the third and the fifth are always given into the custody of the man even if the divorce is caused by the man's violence. 'The children sob and they cry,' she says, and repeats with more emphasis, 'The children sob and cry. It is like tearing the parts of a body apart.'

8

PAIN

I am sitting where I can hear Sopaul as he listens to a woman newly arrived in the camp. It is mid-afternoon, the tropical rain pools and puddles around us. The woman talks and sobs. She weeps as though she will never stop, until her eyes have no more tears.

Her husband was fleeing conscription. They made their way from Battambang to the Thai border carrying their baby and their small child. They met with a unit of soldiers. She doesn't know from which faction. This mother, her children and the man who would not fight, annoyed the soldiers, who surrounded them. One snatched the baby and swung him against a tree trunk. He died with his head battered in. She is shuddering with sobs. She tells it while the rain hammers on our thatch roof. The small son is watching with big eyes, listening to the words recounting the horror he too witnessed. They killed her husband. They left her to walk on alone with this child.

Sopaul listens to her story as she weeps. His voice is comforting, he reaches out to her grief with his eyes. A Cambodian man who upholds tradition should not touch a woman, not even his wife, in public. Sopaul signals to me to come closer and the weeping woman buries her face in the hollow beneath my shoulder, wraps both arms around me and holds tight. Tears soak through tee-shirt to flesh.

PAIN

Sopaul is no stranger to this dark grief. There is a well of pain in his own life. He listens until she really has no more tears.

Ω

A young man, perhaps a soldier, is brought on the back of a bike to MHTH. He is lying on a bench outside the shelter, delivered with no explanation. He has been tortured horribly; by the look of it just this week. He isn't talking. Can't talk or won't talk, we don't know.

I stand looking down at him. He is young, just a boy. I am shocked, too shocked to move. He looks into my face and gropes towards my hand. He holds it tight. He squeezes it and hangs on to it like a lifeline. His lips are swollen and split but he is forming a word. I bend down closer. 'Momma', he says, 'Momma.'

Ω

It is still raining when I reach my wooden house in Ta Phraya. Water swishes beneath its low foundations and runs down to the unpaved road where it pools. The four timber steps to the front door are wet and slippery. I fumble with the key. Rain is thudding on the tin roof and leaking into the kitchen.

There is an easy solution to prevent the house from flooding. The handles of spoons twisted between the floorboards widen the gap in the floor so that what comes through the roof pours down to the stream below the house. I'm adjusting to the domestic chores needed to survive the wet season. It is not cold. It is sheltered. It is home.

I have a gas bottle here. I make hot green tea, light a candle, sit back on my floor cushion and prop another cushion at my back.

WRITING FOR RAKSMEY

The candle glows on the rough timber of the walls, the rafters of the ceiling and the ribs of the house frame. It lights up the bars on the glassless windows and reaches as far as the inside of the tin roof with its smudges of rust. I am looking for my twenty-centimetre-long fat gecko who is sure to be somewhere on the walls or roof. He announces himself, 'Ghe gau.'

Since I am at home tears can stream down my face unchecked.

Tears for the mother and for the child with the big eyes. He will listen again and again to the retelling of the horror that he has witnessed. Tears for the tortured boy. Tears for Momma. Momma is not a word I have heard used in Khmer. Was he Vietnamese? Chinese-Vietnamese? Whoever she is, may she never have to know what has happened to him.

The candle is burning low. I am too restless to go to bed. The faction who did the killing or the faction who did the torture could be the Khmer Peoples' National Liberation Front, of Site 2.

9

CPR

There is an American whose experience and thoughtfulness I esteem even though his unpredictability frustrates me. I met Bob Maat when I first arrived. He was a Jesuit, then, on the edge of this tight community of expatriates in Ta Phraya. He laughingly gave me advice about illnesses I was likely to suffer.

He no longer comes to Site 2; he's taking a year off from that, it is said. Since he has been a constant presence from the earliest days of the border, people wonder what he is thinking. Most international workers come and go. He offers a few words of advice to newcomers, perhaps always half in jest, as in his warning to me. I wonder how many volunteers have come and gone, how many he has welcomed and farewelled during the nine years he has been here.

Nobody expects to see Bob in the usual places, where we gather for meals. Nobody would ever imagine that he would appear at the Friday night Ta Phraya get-togethers where music is strident, drinks ample and images of the week blotted out. However, he is not unnoticed. There is talk and speculation.

It is said that he spent a decade campaigning for human rights for African Americans in the USA. Why this passion for justice and this commitment?

WRITING FOR RAKSMEY

I recall my own path into the Josephites, though not at quite so young an age. It was a response to my deep, inexplicabe awareness of God's love – enough to commit my life to whatever God intended for this planet. Vowed in a time of vision, lived in gritty reality. Gladly though. Is it like this for Bob, I wonder.

In 1979, when the appalling stories of Khmer Rouge atrocities began to be exposed, when survivors were pictured starving, homeless, traumatised at the edge of Thailand, Bob came to the refugee camps. As a Jesuit brother he was already qualified as physician's assistant. He was soon working with the American Refugee Committee in training Cambodians to diagnose and treat TB.

Though he was young, Cambodians called Bob 'Ta'. He was a wise one, a teacher, literally a grandfather. The title referred to more than medical knowledge; he was respected. In 1988, when the violence in these camps was exposed in world media, UNBRO recruited Bob as a Protection Officer. He agreed to take on this resposibility and, if the UN was serious in providing protection for the Cambodians, he was willing to pioneer a new strategy. There were at this time a quarter of a million people needing protection in the camps along the border.

I am told that Bob resigned disillusioned, when resources for protection were so meagre that he belived his role was a farce, a cover-up. He called it a lie.

On a hot afternoon our pathways intersect.

I had wanted to walk alone through the dusty rice field but am glad enough to fall into step with Bob, talking of the crop, the harvest, the heat, the camp.

He tells me that one day he was called to investigate the report of a body found just outside the barbed wire fence of Site 2. He found a middle-aged woman brutally hacked to death. The place where she was attacked was close to people living just inside the barbed wire. It was his responsibility to trace her family. He asked her son-in-law why nobody had reported hearing her screams. 'She's deaf and dumb.'

This haunts him; he sees it as metaphor for the camp. Nobody hears the screams. 'It is a silent scream.' He knew then that he must stop this pretence that the people were protected. He quotes Shakespeare. 'The weight of this sad time we must obey. Speak what we feel, not what we ought to say.' He has no doubts; he will no longer work in Site 2. He has seen too much.

Ω

In one more week it is December 10th, International Human Rights Day. The UN workers suggest that there could be celebrations in the camp. An elephant could be brought in. It would be like giving the people a glimpse of their country; they could celebrate. My Cambodian friends protest. 'We are prisoners in this place and our rights are ignored every day. We should call it "Human Wrongs Day".' No elephant. Speeches instead.

Of all the Human Rights Day speeches, the one that is remembered is the one given by Bob. Hundreds, perhaps thousands of refugees gather to hear. He talks of the harvest which is in full swing outside the barbed wire, where these refugee rice farmers cannot see it. He talks of the struggles for peace, of the need to find peace without violence. War never brings peace. Peace is the way to peace. He finishes by shouting into the sunset, 'Next year, home for the harvest.' The chant is picked up, 'Home for the harvest. Home for the harvest.' It echoes. 'Home for the harvest.'

WRITING FOR RAKSMEY

Ω

We meet in Ta Phraya, a small group of foreign workers and some Cambodians out from the camp for workshops. There must surely be some way to make the silent scream heard. With our mix of contacts in many countries we could get messages out to the world. We will spread up-to-date information through all possible networks in our home countries. We will form a group. Bob doesn't care what the group is called as long as the initials are CPR; it is a life and death situation and seems closer to death. The name will be Coalition for Peace and Reconciliation.

We design a logo, write and collate letters, fold pages, stuff envelopes. Bob will be the spokesperson for this group.

Ω

I read the Asia Watch report about protection at the border:

> The first full-time protection officer was not in place until March 1988 and more staff was not recruited until September of that year. Despite the common belief that only a fraction of incidents ever reached the attention of UNBRO, in the first two years an astonishing number of complaints was recorded, including 792 incidents of beating, 261 incidents of knifing or axing, 101 shootings, 52 assaults by grenade, 57 assaults by shelling or mines, 64 reports of rape or sexual abuse, and 164 suicides. Many of the incidents involved factional administrations, the Thai border units, Task Force 80 and, to a lesser extent, its successor the Displaced Person's Protection Unit (DPPU) ... The first UNBRO protection officer resigned ... returning all his pay checks to UNBRO ... as a protest against the low priority the agency gave to disclosure, advocacy and supervision.

Ω

I am thinking that if good people out there in the world, people with power and influence, could start to understand the dark pit of Cambodian suffering on this border, if they could see it, they would work to change it. Surely. And so, on this Saturday morning, I head through gusts of hot wind to the makeshift Coalition for Peace and Reconciliation office in Ta Phraya.

It is here that we keep folding the news sheets Bob has written and photocopied in Aranyaprathet, stuffing them into the addressed envelopes, trying to keep them clean of sweat and dust, thinking that good people will surely take notice if we keep informing them about what we see and know. As I seal the envelopes I always note the ones addressed to Bob Hawke and to Gareth Evans. Australia should care.

On this Saturday morning Bob Maat tells me that a parcel has arrived from California, via Bangkok. He squats, Thai-farmer style, on a chair and reaches across the table to push aside the bundles of papers, the stacks of envelopes ready to fill, the boxes of addressed mail, the empty Coke cans. He finds the package and hands me a video cassette in a box. He tells me that Ellen Bruno, whom he met here on the Border in the early eighties, produced it. I take the box and turn it over.

It is a documentary filmed in Phnom Penh and called *Samsara: Death and Rebirth in Cambodia*. It is marked 'Special Jury Recognition' Sundance Film Festival. In this cluttered space there is no time to watch it, no projector and, on this particular morning, no electricity. It is my responsibility to view it and find a use for it.

10

SAMSARA

Among my refugee friends in the camp Soeun is the only one with whom I talk of world affairs. I tell him about the video. 'Bring it in here to me,' he says. Within a few days Soeun has a small generator, has linked it to a TV set and the TV to a video player. When the day's work at the Centre For Healing is over he plays *Samsara*, likes it, and tells me about it.

I am intrigued at the ease with which this happened.

KPDR is respected by camp authorities. The Cambodian resistance leaders who control the camp come to this Centre of Healing for relief from their own aches and rashes and sleeplessness. They believe in traditional ways and would rather come here than to camp hospitals controlled by Westerners. Because of this, Phaly and Soeun can often get what they need for their projects. After many small concessions this Centre for Healing in Site 2 South has become an oasis, with water for steam baths and then for tending flower pots, with glass canisters for the herbs, leaves and bark needed for the traditional medicines. There is a sense of normality here that I have not seen anywhere else in Site 2.

When Soeun is ready to show Samsara to me I stay overnight in the Centre. I settle on a floor cushion in candlelight, a guest. Phaly serves me hot tea with fresh jasmine flowers floating on top. She has snipped them from a flower pot in her little garden. They smell of summer holidays.

I picture Phaly as she would have been in Phnom Penh, offering friends all that her income and her husband's income could provide. Her dark hair may have been swept into a chignon, her movements would have been graceful. Now, though I am the only guest, she revels in hospitality. Good things are for sharing. All that she asks of me is friendly companionship: to sit with the family and to watch a movie. We settle down together, entering the world of Cambodia, familiar in memory for Phaly and Soeun, known to me only from reading.

Phaly's son Thero sits beside me. I'm interested in the way that he is navigating young adulthood in this place. He studies, he reads books and is learning English. Most days Thero and I will greet each other with a few words in English, it's good practice for him. Tonight I am glad to have time for a longer conversation.

Thalika, Soeun's nephew, is here too. Souen is sure that both parents of this young man died in the Khmer Rouge time. He has an obligation to give his relative a start in life. Thalika lives in the KPDR compound and has joined the classes for the staff. He has natural talent and enjoys the work.

We hush and settle. Soeun flicks the switches. The twenty-eight minute reel shows life as it was just a few months ago in and around the Cambodian capital, Phnom Penh. Cambodian men and women look into the camera from doorways, from roadsides, from among lush tropical growth. They tell of their suffering, tell of their hopes. There is poetry in word and in earthy images both Buddhist and Khmer: the cycle of birth, of blood then the milk, darkness and light, drought and rain, the spirits of a generation of murdered babies entering into a new generation of babies, killing fields becoming rice fields once more. There is a background narrative that interchanges between ancient prophecy, folklore and dreams. Images of destruction alternate with depictions of beauty, of regeneration, of hope. I am sniffing and wiping my eyes. As it finishes I turn to Soeun watching for his reaction.

Soeun's face is as set and serene as the stone-carved faces in the Angkor temples. He has grasped a message. 'Everyone has suffered; there must be love now.' And then, 'We need to show this film around the camp.'

It will be a challenge. There is of course no theatre. Much of the commentary is in English and very few will understand this. Soeun is not daunted. 'They have a right to see and hear it.' He has thought about how it could be adapted for Site 2.

Cambodians filmed on the streets of Phnom Penh speak Khmer, of course. For viewers in America there are subtitles in English. We can get rid of these. Everyone here speaks Khmer. On the other hand, the commentary spoken in English adds reflection to what the people say: it is poetic. Soeun thinks that if I could transcribe the English content his friend Barnabas would translate it to Khmer. 'Maybe,' I say, 'Maybe.'

Soeun's plan is to produce this in time for the next Human Rights Day. He will involve the leaders of the Centre for Healing in Site 2 North MHTH together with the Site 2 South KPDR with this project. They will see its value; they have the heart for it.

Day after day during spare lunchtime moments in the camp I cycle to KPDR to wind and rewind the tape, writing down each word as I hear a woman and a man in the USA speak it in English. I cycle back to MHTH in the red-laterite glare of noon, wondering whether the effort is worthwhile.

Barnabas is the most optimistic refugee I have met; nothing can daunt him. As fast as I transcribe the English he arrives on a bicycle to translate it to Khmer.

Phaly is scouting the camp for actors, a woman and a man, to record the script he is writing. Many artists and actors have sought refuge at the border. Phaly can talk to the powerful and those who have grown rich in this place. She is using all of her persuasion to cover the cost of producing the entire film in Khmer. A man and a woman who are recommended for the Khmer commentary watch the film. Stirred by what they see and hear neither will accept the payment that is offered. They persuade musicians in the camp to provide the music behind their voices.

'This film is about healing,' Nee says.

'Where will you show it?' I ask. Soeun, Nee and Phaly have talked about this; they will show it from the Ute. It will be possible to set up a generator and cassette player in the tray of the Ute and TV screens on a platform above the cabin. There is enough talent in Site 2 to manage this; technicians who qualified and practiced in Phnom Penh before Khmer Rouge times want to be part of it. Soeun has friends and friends of friends to find the skills that are needed.

All I will need to do on December 10th is to have the Ute in the camp by 6 am so that the equipment can be set up for a first showing at 8 am. Every hour on the hour, Samsara in Khmer will be shown in a different section of Site 2.

Notices are hand-written and taped to walls close to where people queue for their ration of rice or of water. Samsara, a film in Cambodian language about Cambodian people, will be shown in this Section at

10 am on Human Rights Day, December 10th.' The route between each showing is carefully planned: this will be the venue at 9 am, this at 10 am, and this at 11 am. There will of course be no charge. The audience can stand or squat or sit on the ground in any of these open spaces.

$$\Omega$$

On Human Rights Day, as soon as it is light, the Ute is parked in a small clearing in the camp. I am standing watching as it is transformed for the mobile cinema.

People around us are awakening as on any other December morning. It is the coolest season of the year. A fresh smell rises from the earth. Women squat to swish loose dust and insects from the thresholds of their huts; families share a toothbrush and a little water, brushing and gargling noisily; dogs bark; the first pushbike taxis trundle past.

Carpenters fit a wooden platform on the cabin of the Ute. Technicians position four TV sets onto the platform and secure them. They load a video player and generator into the Ute's tray and link each TV to the player. By now children sense something unusual happening. They cluster around to watch, hugging themselves in the cool air, smelling of their crowded sleep, sniffing and rubbing their eyes. 'Okay. Bye-bye.' Some cling to my skirt, nestling in with their runny noses. The carpenters adjust a canopy to shield the TV screens from glare. Technicians tune the speakers.

Leaders from both of the Centres for Healing are waiting and ready; once the roadshow is set up it will be their responsibility to keep it moving on time and to ensure that those who are watching are cared for. 'Many people watching this will remember sad things. We need to be on standby.'

The first showing is at the margin of the camp. Neighbours surround the Ute. There is a screen to the north, the south, the east and the west. People encircle this astounding display to see what is happening. Wherever they choose to sit or stand they can see a screen. The men, mostly off-duty soldiers, lift small children on to their shoulders. Women knot their kramas into a sling to hold their babies. Children wriggle through the throng to gain a better view. Among the jostling audience most are seeing a TV for the first time; they are fascinated. Those who recognise a landmark in Phnom Penh call out in excitement. They lift their children and explain to them, 'This is your country.' Some laugh. Others weep quietly.

After the half-hour showing the Ute moves slowly to the next site. Many in the audience follow to watch again and again. Word spreads. The crowd swells to several hundred. I leave the driving to Soeun and walk with the people to catch their conversation. Some recount the horror of Khmer Rouge times. Some touch hope as if it is an unfamiliar garment being fitted. The day is already hot. I am wiping away sweat with my krama and using it to shield my head and face from the sun. I watch each viewing.

One image grabs the attention of many. The camera zooms to a message chalked in Khmer characters on a crumbling wall beside an empty opening where once a door was fitted. There is no house behind; the doorway leads to a vacant space. The chalked Khmer message reads, 'Husband, if you are alive come to the house of my aunt near Psar Thmey. I will wait for you there.' The audience becomes still. I watch the faces, the furrowed forehead, the clenched lower lip.

Each watcher has left a familiar doorway, or a hut in a village. Each has some loved one who may be alive or may be dead.

For the 5 pm showing, the tenth of the day, we are in the centre of the camp, the margin between south and north, exhausted and exhilarated. Even this broad space at the crossroads close to the UNBRO office is not large enough for the crowd to spread out; people are packed shoulder to shoulder. Some have followed for most of the day, some have heard news of the film from earlier viewers, some have been waiting for the scheduled time in this place.

Shadows are long, the sun is low in the sky, any small movement of air is a welcome gift as the day cools. I watch from among the tight-packed throng. Though I am tall I need to crane to view the screen in the distance and to estimate the numbers in this biggest audience of the day. There may be thousands of people packed close together filling the space. It is impossible to count. The man beside me has hoisted to his shoulders a friend who has had both legs amputated. Both men worry that I may not have a good enough view. 'Can you see? You need to see. This is our country.'

A man pushes through the crowd ignoring the screen, looking for me. 'Mr Lay Khec wants to see you, follow me.' This is a command, not an invitation. My throat tightens. I try in vain to look unconcerned. Mr Lay Khec, whom I have never met, is widely feared both as an army chief and as the leader of Site 2 North; he has a reputation for being ruthless. I squeeze through the throng, breathing deeply, trying to form answers to questions I can't imagine.

Mr Lay Khec makes no greeting. He sits behind a table, the authority. I stand just inside his door, called in to be reprimanded. 'This film should not be shown. The people should not be seeing this.'

'But it's their country,' I say. As the words leave my mouth I know that my reply is both lame and naive. Site 2 exists to oppose the political and military forces in Phnom Penh. Phnom Penh is the enemy.

'It is a security risk', he says. 'Anybody could toss a hand grenade into this packed crowd. It would be carnage.' This sounds like a threat; he has the power to cause a grenade attack and I can feel his anger. On the other hand, he is also in a better position than I am to gauge danger.

If his purpose is for me to feel responsible he has succeeded. I push to the centre of the crowd towards the Ute where Soeun, Bora, Thalika and Nee are clustered together, concentrating on the technology. I tug for Nee's attention. 'Mr Lay Khec says we should stop. He says that the crowd is out of control. Someone could throw a hand grenade.'

We are close to the boom of the amplifiers but he has heard what I said. 'This is not a political movie. If the people are not permitted to think of their own story and to see images of their own homeland then we truly are frogs in the bottom of a deep well.'

The show finishes. The slow-moving Ute turns to the south for a final dusk event at the rice distribution field in Site 2 South. Many supporters crowd around and behind it. I am swept into following what I fear may be a disaster, carnage, retribution, revenge. I am clammy and jerky with fear. The sky is pink now. I believe danger is real but am powerless to stop the surge that has started. The crowd is elated as if suddenly united with a purpose.

I saw *Les Miserables* before I left Australia. What I am watching feels as unreal as a stage setting. Women and men, surely strangers to each other, talk together while they walk shoulder to shoulder on the red road I have cycled along so often. 'It is the music of a people who will not be slaves again.' That is it.

I concentrate on one thought, 'Soeun, Nee, Bora and Thalika understand the cost of dissent more than I ever will.'

The pink sky softens to grey. I know that these men, my friends, my pupils for a short time, are strong and independent. I am walking behind.

Ω

There is a final showing, there is orderly dismantling of the equipment, I drive back to Ta Phraya. The events of the day crowd my thoughts through a restless night. At first light I abandon the effort to sleep and quieten into meditation.

The Josephite tradition has the words '… a call to encounter God in the many faces of the poor, to learn from them, to receive from them, to support them in their struggle for justice and equity. It is an experience of God … painful … disturbing …'

After coffee and a mango I wait to catch a bus to Bangkok for a scheduled meeting with COERR, my mind hovering around the encounter with Lay Khec, replaying it, realising that it is a conversation that ought not be left unfinished. I crumple the bus ticket and drive back to Site 2.

Khec seems to half expect me. This time I sit down without being invited. He glares at me across his desk. We move into the conversation we had barely started. I am adding the heated words that have shaped in my mind overnight. Becoming calmer we embroider with anecdotes from our experience. I guess that we were born at about the same time.

'Right.'

'So you became a teacher in a primary school in the countryside before you were twenty years old?'

'So did I.' Our ideals were so similar then. Our opinions are so different now. 'So?'

'So?'

'You didn't see your family killed in front of you,' he says.

11

TO SEE INSIDE CAMBODIA

Lud says, 'We should see Cambodia. We ought to go, you know.'

Khmer friends hear of this. 'You need to see it, and then you will understand.'

'Try to spend a long quiet time with my mother.'

'I have nobody left but I want you to stand outside the prison where we were held and take a photo of it. Or if you would rather, take a photo of the pagoda across the road from the prison.'

'My mother and father are very poor and they have suffered so much. Perhaps their hair will be white. Their house is easy to find. I will draw you a map. Try to take a photo of them.'

The very mention of a visit brings tears. Phaly sums it up, 'Tell them I will soon be home.' She has never before spoken to me so urgently. I want to do this for her.

'Home for the harvest', I am thinking. Home for the next harvest. If we go soon it will be harvest time when we arrive.

$$\Omega$$

There is, of course, no safe land route from the border into Cambodia. To enter Cambodia through Pochentong Airport we need a visa. Lud has heard that a Cambodian man, a double amputee who lives in a village near the border, has contacts. We take the risk. He hands back our passports stamped with a visa.

The plane is small. It flies low. I see, through early morning mist, sights we were told to expect: sugar palms rising up from the fields exactly as the children in the camp had been taught to draw them, the Tonle Sap with fishing boats throwing nets on sparkling waters, the braided Mekong Delta. I press my face against the window of the plane swallowing the view, savouring it.

We walk out from the airport into a ragged city where women and men, so like our friends in the camp, are working to earn a wage. They are in control of their lives. Their expressions, their mannerisms, the cadence of their voices are all familiar. The difference is that they are free.

Our 'man from the ministry' waits to meet us as we arrive at the airport. We expect this. The government in Phnom Penh is still suspicious of foreigners. He gives us a choice of two hotels in which to stay. We choose the Monorom, which proves to be too expensive for us so we move to the Asie. 'Our man' visits us each night. We chat to him about what we have been doing and presume he reports back to his government department.

$$\Omega$$

Slowly a few small doubts, like ripples from pebbles dropped into smooth water, ruffle the image we want to see.

When we stroll unintentionally into a rally on the street, 'our man' appears on a motorbike within minutes and whisks us way. When we stop outside Phsar Tmey to photograph the sign warning that rocket launchers, AK-47s and grenades must be left outside this market, a man passing close to us whispers, 'Site 2 is a small prison, this country is one big prison.' Once we see a woman running frantically through a crowd pursued by a well-dressed man. Nobody helps her.

$$\Omega$$

The Asie hotel is adequate: there is one large bed in our room, there is a dipper shower and squat toilet in the adjoining closet.

At first light each morning we stand at our third-floor window and watch as the streets and alleys below stir into life. The footpaths and the rundown lane opposite our window are lined with people lying side by side. They stir from sleep, fold the cardboard or paper they had used for a bed, urinate in some corner of the laneway, comb their hair. Parents attend to their children as the light grows stronger. They tidy the space they have used for sleeping. Then they slip away.

The peeling paint and crumbling stucco of the popular central market up the road to our left, Phsar Tmey, absorbs the pink-gold of the sunrise. Soon after six each morning Lud and I walk through the town, through slush and garbage, past beggars, past mothers with small babies, past amputees in army uniform.

When the sun is higher in the sky we visit the families of our friends; the joy we bring with the letters we carry is always mixed with sadness. We listen to stories, share the news that families would want to hear, take photos and offer to return to collect letters to bring back to the camp.

Phaly's mother welcomes us but her father is on his deathbed. He is begging for his daughter, not for two strangers, foreigners who bring letters and photos but cannot bring Phaly.

TO SEE INSIDE CAMBODIA

Ω

Close to the end of our eighteen days we still have last promises to keep. We want to visit the families of Nee and of Sopaul in Choeuteal, a village in Svey Rieng Province one hundred and fifty kilometres south-east of Phnom Penh. There are two problems: we require permission to travel to the provinces and we need transport.

Our man from the ministry offers to take us, provided we can leave at 5.30 in the morning, be back in Phnom Penh by nightfall, and pay for the petrol for his car. He will be our taxi driver and guide. With some disquiet about leading this man to families with connections to the camp of the opposition faction, we agree. We know that our other family visits have already been observed, yet families have always seemed genuinely grateful that we have come.

Beyond the Neak Leung ferry crossing, close to the point where the rough highway enters into the Svey Rieng province, there is a vendor selling sugarcane juice. We stop to quench our thirst, to chat with this man, and to enquire about the route to our destination. He knows immediately; the teacher in Choeuteal village was his schoolmaster. He tells us that this teacher was a good man killed by the Khmer Rouge simply because he was a teacher. If we could wait a minute for him to put on a clean shirt he would be honoured to guide us to the widow.

Thirty minutes further along the rough road we turn right into a dirt track, then swerve and bump towards Choeuteal. Tall bamboos flourish on each side of the track. Here and there small, thatched-roof timber houses come into sight, at first widely separated then clustered into a tight group. The bamboo is now so dense that it forms an archway across the track. This is the village.

WRITING FOR RAKSMEY

The car slows and stops in front of a one-roomed timber house on stilts. Outside the house, close to the edge of the track, there is a 'shop' made of a bamboo platform on stilts with three bamboo walls, a thatch roof and a bench with a small selection of sweet drinks and coconuts. This kiosk is about two metres wide and three metres long; it is the kind of meeting place where neighbours gather when they have a few riel to spend on a treat.

We see the woman behind the counter, a short, slim, nut-brown woman with her dark hair cut straight, just covering her ears. She looks at the slowing car, a rare sight so far from the main road, snatches a krama to swab her face and rushes to greet us. Ignoring the men she clings to Lud and me. She has seen our photo in a message from her son Nee. 'Is he dead? Is he hurt? Is he here?'

She holds me as we climb stiffly out of the car, leads me up to the platform of her small shop and places two low stools where we can sit together. Her questions come faster than I can frame answers in Khmer. 'Is he good? Is he studying? He has a wife? What is she like? His children, my grandchildren, what are they like?' I carry photos and have stories to tell. This middle-aged woman with deep lines of sadness and fun across her face is hungry for her son. I am a direct connection. We sit on the two stools, leaning towards each other.

People flock from other houses in the village. News from the border camps is important to many of them. Young village men remove the walls and roof of the little shop so that Nee's mother and I are on a platform like a makeshift stage, where we can be seen and heard. She seems to be aware of nothing other than this flimsy link with her son. Lud has a bag of balloons and is teaching the children how to blow them up. Balloons are bursting, children are squealing. It is a carnival.

Sopaul's family live close by. They have had no direct contact with Sopaul for nine years. He had feared that one or both of his parents might have died. Lud goes to them, taking Sopaul's letters, and they prepare messages to send back to assure him that they are alive and well.

Time is slithering away. The man from the ministry decides that we should begin the journey back to the capital immediately. Without a word Nee's mother folds a clean sarong and krama, tucks a toothbrush and a comb into the fold and climbs into the car with the sugar cane vendor, the man from the ministry and the two barang. She has no intention of saying goodbye until she has finished asking questions.

Ω

At the Asie the bed is large enough for the three of us. During restless nights there are more questions. 'Is he good? Is he good?' There is not enough language between us to enable me to be sure that she can comprehend what has happened in all of these years, that this eldest boy of hers has led a group of refugees to the border through minefields, that he has shivered and sweated with malaria longing to die, that he has become a man. I keep saying, 'Yes, he is good.'

Each morning Nee's mother showers with the dipper, dabs her hair and her body with her krama, rinses the krama and hangs it at the window to dry in the heat of the sun. She smooths back her hair and tucks it behind her ears. As it dries a few locks bend towards her face a little. What I notice most is her simplicity. She has a daily routine that she follows, she will always be neat and clean. Though there is a mirror in the room she never checks her appearance. She meets life as she is.

WRITING FOR RAKSMEY

I wonder which stories of her son would cause her to be anxious and which would cause her to feel proud of him. Many times Nee's mother says to me 'He still needs a mother, be a second mother to him.' She speaks no English but I keep trying to assure her in Khmer that she is the mother he needs; he needs to come home.

12

FACING THE FEAR

Theary has responded to an invitation to speak at a conference in Sydney sponsored by a partnership between the Josephite Sisters at St Margaret's Hospital and the Refugee Council of Australia. 'The Never-Ending Story', they name it.

I stand waiting in the old Bangkok airport to meet her on her return. Because those detained in Site 2 have only the passport of the coalition of the resistance factions, more is often needed. She is carrying papers prepared by Australian officials in Bangkok. It takes courage to do what she has done. I have had messages from Sydney that her presentation and her presence have been important to the conference. This is reassuring. I try to imagine the challenge of sudden transition from Site 2 to Australia. She left the camp with just a small shoulder bag and a change of clothes. Here in a department store in Bangkok we bought warm clothes to prepare for cold Sydney weather. She chose a pair of high-heeled shoes, her first. She carried in her shoulder bag a typed copy of the paper she would give.

The arrivals screen indicates that her Qantas flight has landed almost on time. There is a surge of excitement among those who wait to greet the passengers. I'm excited too. I watch the first travellers come through with their business class luggage. No need to expect Theary among these. I wait as the arrivals through the customs doors dwindle to one or two at a time, then the occasional one. When there are no more I go to the enquiry desk. 'There is nobody else,' the man behind the glass window says. 'There must be. I know for sure that she caught the plane.' I know that my voice sounds high and anxious. He turns away from me. 'Sorry, there is nothing we can do. There will be no more passengers.' The window closes, the blind is pulled down.

Lights throughout the terminal dim. The small band of Thai workers who remain pay no attention to my escalating panic. They push big oblong orange mops across the bare stretches of terrazzo floor calling to each other as the long day's work is finishing. The customs officers begin to close their gates.

I am desperate to do something. The only thing I can think to do is to walk into the customs area through an exit, looking neither right nor left, believing that if I keep a steady calm pace the polite Thai officials, probably all men, will not know what to do with me: an 'older' barang woman who seems to be deaf.

Ahead is a long, dim corridor edged by benches. At the end of it I can see Theary encircled by men in uniforms. She looks up and sees me. She breaks away from the circle. We run towards each other with open arms. I hold her tightly with no plan of what to do next. At this moment, for the first time since I was a child, my nose begins to bleed, not gently but in great spurts.

In an instant Theary becomes the nurse in total charge of the patient. The men who had been questioning her and certainly should have been dealing severely with me follow her commands without hesitation. She speaks with authority and, besides, there is a lot of blood around. 'Pull that bench over here; we need to make a bed. Get me cold water. Well if there is no water get me cold Coke. Hurry. Lie down. Lean your head back. Hold the bridge of your nose.' Theary bends over me, mopping up blood and whispers, 'It is so good that this happened.'

$$\Omega$$

Late one afternoon, as I should be leaving the camp, Tolla calls me over to where he sits talking to a slender young woman with a wounded eye and badly bruised face. In each arm she holds a squirming baby boy, twins of about one year old. As is usual the babies are not clothed, and as is also usual one is trying to suck at her breast. The mother, despite her injuries, has the air of one who has matters well in hand. Tolla is practical and exact, this is the way he tells me her story.

The woman became pregnant even though breast-feeding, but miscarried three days ago after a severe beating from her husband. Onlookers ran to get the Khmer police, a force becoming effective in the camp, and the husband was gaoled. While he awaited trial there was nobody to 'bail him out' but herself. He is a powerful man, a commander in the army. There is immense pressure for her to take him from the gaol and rescue him from the course the new justice committee should take. This afternoon two of his army friends threatened her with a gun. Firearms and grenades are readily available and vengeance all too easy.

I hear this young woman saying to Tolla that she cannot always run. She has to turn and face the fear.

$$\Omega$$

WRITING FOR RAKSMEY

The weekend is sometimes an opportunity for a friendly visit to families of the people I work among during the week. I drive into the camp on a Sunday morning and sense that something is amiss. A glance at Thalika's worried face confirms that this is so. He needs time to talk to me alone. We move to a bench outside, assuring his wife that I will come inside to be with the family later.

'Something very bad happened here last night. Soeun says I should tell you about it.' This sounds official. On Saturday night there would have been no foreigners in the camp and I am the first on this Sunday morning. I wriggle back on the bench into the meagre shade of the tattered thatch roofing and reach into my bag for notebook and pencil.

Thalika speaks English well. He is a student in the advanced course of counselling. His report of what he saw and heard is methodical.

About sixty bandits wearing a variety of pieces of KPNLF and KR uniform, armed with AK-47s, rocket launchers and mortars, entered Site 2 from the south. He points in the direction. It all happened close to where we now sit. The bandits were challenged by a Khmer policeman and retaliated by opening fire and moving deeper into the camp, still shooting.

KPDR was adjacent to the worst of the violence. When Phaly and Soeun heard the first firing at about 7.30 pm they immediately gathered patients and their families into the bunkers and under the traditional-medicine drying racks. There was a message from the American Refugee Committee Hospital across the road that one of their workers was hit in the mouth with shrapnel and was bleeding profusely. They ran to the hospital and saw scenes of panic. The injured of the neighbourhood were being brought to the hospital by their families. Other families were taking shelter in the hospital grounds where the electric light from the hospital generator gave a feeling of safety. Soeun helped to organise the ambulances. There were approximately twenty wounded, eight critically so. Two children were dead, another died in the hospital.

As we talk an Australian television crew arrives in the camp, smelling news. They had heard in Ta Phraya that an Australian could be found here this morning. Now they have the unexpected opportunity of a much bigger story. Thalika looks into the camera and tells what he saw. I hear the cameraman from Sydney say, 'This is talent.' He nods to me, 'Thanks luv.'

$$\Omega$$

Bora has a worry. He comes to MHTH to talk it over with Nee, as he often does. Nee is just over thirty; Bora, the impulsive one, is not yet twenty. I have watched Bora acting like a seventeen-year-old, holding a piece of broken mirror while he combs his hair into style and turns up his collar to a jaunty angle. When he accepts responsibilities too heavy for his age Nee is like an elder brother for him. This afternoon the worry is about a prisoner in the Site 2 lockup. Nee draws me into the conversation; MHTH is caring for this prisoner's depressed wife and young children.

In his role on the UNBRO Protection Team, Bora has learned that there are plans to move the prisoner to a gaol in another border camp. 'Prisoners sent there are lynched.'

Bora has some reason to dislike the prisoner but he cannot stand by and see this injustice done. His handsome young face collapses into furrows as I have seen it do before. I see the two talking together, Nee the responsible father of a family, Bora passionate and reckless. Nee is warning that the commanders planning the transfer are powerful. Though he is not brushing aside the concern he is urging caution.

There is no rule of law to prevent this extradition. 'Jum merl sun,' says Nee. Wait and see for a while.

In the dark hours of the night Bora beats on Nee's door. No time to wait. The authorities of the other camp have arrived and are packing the belongings of the prisoner. The wife and two children will be next to be hassled.

Tolla, who is on duty, understands this crisis. Without hesitation the three rush together to the prison, alerting the Cambodians at the UNBRO office as they pass by. 'He is surely guilty of a crime,' they say, 'but it is not a crime that deserves capital punishment.' They are ridiculed and called 'dogs of the barang', a wounding insult. They stand their ground. A Thai camp officer with everything to lose and nothing to gain takes his place beside them. They know that they are risking their lives, they presume the prisoner may already have been taken away. They do not budge.

Without them knowing it the decision is delayed until morning. In the early morning it is reversed.

When I come into the camp for the start of work there is a message for me to go to them. They are still standing watch at the prison, believing that their effort has been in vain. 'The first time I stood up for another Cambodian,' says Nee with quite a degree of exaggeration, 'they ridiculed me. I failed.'

But they had not failed.

Jo Blanco, a Jesuit fresh from the Philippines People Power movement, speaks at a meeting in the camp later that same day. 'When people allow oppression to continue they are already destroyed in the process. There has to be a way found where people are liberators of themselves, a way that is absolutely respectful of human dignity.

Violent ways are not bringing peace. But non-violent ways of resisting will demand a great price.'

Tolla, Bora and Nee understand what he is saying.

After the meeting we stand talking in groups. Jo overhears Nee saying that he was patronised and treated like a small child when he tried to stand up for the rights of another Cambodian. Jo joins our group. 'So I share this day with you. Of course you paid the price. You will always pay the price. But for many years now you have suffered with no result. This time your suffering has meaning.'

I am listening, believing that what is said is true. I am swamped with foreboding.

These young men are well aware of the cost of standing against injustice. They are willing to take risks. I cherish them and I am afraid. The direction they are taking is full of risk.

$$\Omega$$

It is rainy season again. The clouds have not yet massed, the midday heat is searing. As we shelter in some sparse shade on the MHTH block Nee and I are reflecting on all that is happening in the Centre. He begins to talk about his own life.

'I was a frog in the bottom of a deep well. The frog could only see darkness.'

'Yes, I remember that time.'

'After a long, long time the frog saw a little bit of light at the top.'

'I know.'

'Then the frog began to turn into a bird. It could fly.'

We sit together, knowing that this is so. 'You are flying now?' I ask.

'My wings are still wet,' he says. 'Blow on them.'

13

THE BEGINNING OF THE ENDING

In Ta Phraya we cluster around a radio listening for all the news we can hear.

In October 1991, in Paris, the four Cambodian factions ratify Agreements with the United Nations. This news has been awaited for a long time. Until the first election can be held in Cambodia, the United Nations will share responsibility with a group of twelve Cambodian faction leaders: six from inside the country and six from the coalition of resistance forces from the border, FUNCINPEC, KPNLF and the Khmer Rouge. This governing body will be known as the Cambodian Supreme National Council, the SNC.

The Accords are signed. Each party to the signing chooses those who will represent it on the SNC. Word spreads through the camp.

The United Nations High Commission for Refugees has silk-screen banners made so that even those who cannot read will be able to imagine what is to happen. Men and women stand in front of the banners. They point to this and that. The images are large and brightly coloured; people debate the meaning of each detail.

There is a bus. Painted on the side of the bus is a logo with the initials 'UN' and the symbol of two hands forming a sheltering roof above a human figure. A wreath of leaves is painted around this symbol. On top of the bus are piled many striped plastic bags, the tough kind with two handles and a zip for closure. This is luggage. In front of the vehicle is a small signpost with 'Cambodia' lettered in Khmer. At the front door of the bus is a man with a clipboard. He is obviously checking the names of people who stand in a long queue waiting to climb onboard. There are women, men and children of all ages. There are two people without legs: one on crutches, one in a wheelchair. The queue is orderly; controlled by men with the UNHCR logo on their shirts. Behind the bus you can distinguish a truck with the same UNHCR logo painted on the door and the bonnet. It is laden with more striped bags and a bicycle. There is a poster in Khmer and English: 'WHEN THERE IS PEACE IN CAMBODIA THE UN WILL HELP YOU TO RETURN TO YOUR COUNTRY SAFELY AND WITH DIGNITY.'

My friends talk about every detail of this message. Can they dare to believe this? Can they dare not to?

Ω

News from inside Cambodia is ominous.

In November, one month after the signing, Son Sann, a member of the SNC representing KPNLF, and Khieu Samphan, representing the Khmer Rouge, fly into Phnom Penh to congratulate Norodom Sihanouk, who has returned to Cambodia from China. The refugees in Site 2 know Mr Son Sann well. He controls this camp.

Powerful people in the camp already have a video of the television coverage of what happened.

As soon as Son Sann and Khieu Samphan reach the Phnom Penh villa that is prepared for them, hundreds of men and women, some armed with hatchets, surround it. The TV footage shows the mob tearing down the fence and swarming into the house with police and soldiers making only half-hearted attempts to hold them back. Eyewitnesses stand gawking at Khieu Samphan lying by a metal cupboard with blood streaming from his head. Though many police and soldiers are present only a few make an attempt to fend off attackers. The mob shouts 'Kill. Kill. Kill. Kill him. Kill him.' They string a wire noose from a ceiling fan. A veteran international photographer, his hand shaking against his microphone, says, 'I thought he was going to be torn apart. They were crazy in there.'

Eventually the bloodied Khieu Samphan and Sonn Sann are escorted to the airport. It is reported that they have been under siege for five hours, part of that time locked in a cupboard. They leave Phnom Penh on the same day that they arrived.

On the streets of Site 2 people talk and worry. 'Khieu Samphan is an old man.'

'An old man treated like that with blood running down his face. Tchk. Tchk. Tchk.'

What will happen when scores of thousands pour into Cambodia from a KPNLF camp?

$$\Omega$$

For years there have been dreams of what the move back to Cambodia would be like. People would dance and sing, it was thought. There would be peace. There would be land to share.

When the time comes it happens like this: there is no popular celebration, the camps simply close. Whether or not it is safe for families to return there will be no refuge in Thailand. One of the

THE BEGINNING OF THE ENDING

Agreements signed in Paris set out the terms of repatriation: everybody will be back in Cambodia for the election in 1993. In workplaces, at crossroads, in the never-ending queues for rice or water, wherever people gather in Site 2, I hear the talk.

'Our village is a battlefield. There is no place to go home to.'

'We have no relatives alive. We no longer have a house; we have heard squatters have taken over. We cannot imagine where we will go.'

'We left our village because it was dangerous for us there. The danger has not changed.'

'I have always been a farmer but how can I live and feed my family if I have no land?'

In the streets and neighbourhoods of Site 2, families watch as registration is organised. They expect that there will be a ballot for the first departures. Some hope to return as quickly as possible, trusting UNHCR to settle them in a safe place far away from the KPNLF. Some are afraid for their lives and wonder how to resist return. Some are willing enough to go but have no idea where they can find welcome or how they can survive. Many are convinced that there is no possibility of peace. They will settle as close to the Thai border as they are able: refuge in Thailand will be needed again.

Everybody has a choice to make. At first UNHCR offers two hectares of land for each family: Option A. When it is realised that there will not be enough land available they offer Option B: instead of two hectares of land the family could have timber cut and ready for the frame of a small house. The family would be responsible for the roof and the walls and inside partitions if they wanted these. They would be given this house kit at a reception centre in Cambodia and would transport it to wherever they chose. Many wonder where they could erect a house frame. For some there might be the possibility that the UNHCR could have an area of land where people from the camps could erect their house frame. The many widows with small children shrug their shoulders. This Option B has countless challenges, so option C is offered: there could be $50 for each adult and $25 for each child. The family could work out the housing and the 'income generation' for themselves.

Eventually there is an Option D: instead of any other benefit there could be a kit of 'tools of trade' – carpentry tools, perhaps, or a sewing machine. If this is taken there will remain the problem of housing and the need for money to start a small business.

I stand among the crowd wondering what I would choose.

Everybody will be entitled to a rice ration for 400 days. If they settle near enough to a UN rice distribution centre they will not starve during the first year back in their country. Everybody will be eligible for transport by bus back to a reception centre in the north, or to near Phnom Penh or in the south of their country.

'Rolls Royce ride back to nothing,' somebody mutters.

Conversation among our friends is about decisions.

$$\Omega$$

Some students from the advanced class at MHTH gather for Saturday morning tutorials. They meet in a relatively quiet place at the edge of the camp away from the usual teaching spaces. They are equal in skill and experience and keen to share insights. I enjoy these Saturday mornings. This is far from rote learning. Now there is lively chatter about ways to respond to the choices that will shape their futures.

THE BEGINNING OF THE ENDING

Thalika, Thavy, Nee, Ty and Soeun know that the suffering of others mirrors their own. It is worth shaping a unit of teaching around what is keeping them awake at night.

The topic is about choices, the decisions that everyone must make. They all remember suffering endured as a result of choices made in the past.

'When those young Khmer Rouge soldiers pointed the guns and ordered us out of Phnom Penh I went immediately. Immediately. I never saw my father again.'

'When I reached here I could have pretended to be Vietnamese. I speak the language. After that I would have a chance to get to Panat Nikhom and be safe but would at the same time risk being sent off into Vietnam.'

'We decided which guide to pay to take us through the minefields. We decided. And he was not a good guide. Our little girls died.'

'I hated coming to the camp. I missed everyone. But if I didn't come here I would have been in the army. Since I did come here I have suffered a lot but I have learned a lot.'

Thalika has made a string of decisions, with no parents to guide him. He avoided army conscription by ensuring that his English language skills and clerical skills were useful in the camp. There was nothing he could do to prevent his brother being conscripted. He heard news that his brother was paralysed, probably paraplegic, in a military base far from Site 2. He gathered information and enlisted help from foreign workers so that his brother could be brought to Site 2. He married a wife who could care for his brother as well as the young children of the family.

The Saturday class starts to see a pattern in the decisions. Sometimes there is no choice. You are simply forced or obliged to act.

The choices they regret most are those they made with not enough facts. Everybody agrees with this. Ty puts words on what they all realise. You can live with a forced choice between things that are all dangerous, things that are all bad, if you know enough facts in advance.

$$\Omega$$

Soeun and Nee know what to do. They will campaign to have refugees represented in the planning meetings for the repatriation and will work to ensure that the facts are shared and understood.

As the UN is securing a road from Aranyaprathet through Poipet to Battambang, then to Phnom Penh, Ty will go by taxi back to his village, leaving his family in the camp until he knows what the choices would mean.

Thalika has heavy family responsibilities now. But he will do his best to use his skills in English, in counselling and in computers to win some job needed for the repatriation.

$$\Omega$$

The repatriation planning meetings in Bangkok are held in the elegant venue of a club in the city. They are attended by UN officials, Thai government representatives, Thai Army officers and International NGOs. By the good efforts of Father Bunlert, Nee and Soeun are permitted to attend, provided they don't speak. We are seated at tables with starched white tablecloths while waiters bring jugs of iced water.

THE BEGINNING OF THE ENDING

The three of us sit together listening while plans are set in place. At the morning tea break Soeun and Nee eat cake, drink coffee and give me their advice.

'Tell them that those bus rides will be the first ride in a motor vehicle that most of these people have ever had. They should make preparations for travel sickness.'

'Village leaders and commune leaders will say they have land for returnees but how will the returnees keep the land after the UN has gone?'

'We have patients who are psychotic. They will be on medication all the way to the reception centre. How will their families manage after that?'

'Tell them that our teams are ready to help with vulnerable people during the repatriation. Our own families would be willing to wait until last.'

'Where will the land be? What about landmines?'

Gradually the two men realise that UNHCR is making forced choices too. Prince Sihanouk says publicly the words that need saying. 'We don't have peace, just a piece of paper.'

The problem is that within nine months, three-hundred-and-sixty-thousand people need to be moved back to Cambodia, at the rate of ten thousand a week, to be in-country and registered in time for the 1993 elections. Sixteen thousand of those to be moved will be amputees and, as well, there will be pregnant women, the seriously ill, the frail elderly and the newborn. Despite the signing of peace, battles are still being fought between Phnom Penh and the Khmer Rouge.

Soeun, Nee and I talk about these things during the long drive back to the camp from the meetings in Bangkok. Inside the fence of

Site 2 we notice a sight we have often seen. A young mother sits on a bamboo bed, holding her newborn child in one hand and tenderly pours a dipper of cool water over the baby and through the slats in the bed. We turn to each other. 'They will be going too.'

$$\Omega$$

Ty returns from his taxi journey. He has travelled south to his village near Oudong in Cambodia, crammed in a small car with eight other passengers, stopping at checkpoints to pay bribes on the way. It was a risky ride. He needs to tell us the details.

'It was sixteen hours. We were bumping and moving from one side of the road to the other. When the car bumps into a rut your head or your shoulder or your arm hits the roof or the window of the car. We all had bruises. The day was getting dark and as we went along some things looked familiar but I was not sure whether this was the place to get out and walk to my village. I knew the others were beginning to be impatient with me so I got out. I asked the first people I met. Was I right? Was my village close? They told me yes it was close, I should walk in the direction of the Wat on top of the hill.

'I came to the edge of the village and I was amazed. I was astounded. People called my name, they remembered me, they stood in a circle around me. I looked at the faces, they were all older than me, they would have watched me from when I was a small child until I grew up and had to run off to the border. They remembered me better than I remembered them.

'A couple of them ran to tell my mother but I had so many tears that I did not notice this. All the way in the taxi I had been telling myself to control my heart but now tears were streaming down my face. I didn't see my mother coming. I just felt her arms around me. She held me for a long time. When I stood back so that I could see her face she fell to the ground weeping.'

As soon as the official repatriation begins Ty and his family move out of Site 2 back to his mother's village near Oudong.

Ω

The two Centres for Healing are busy. People who can normally live fairly calmly in this tough place are stressed because of the decisions they face. Adding to the stress, 'bandit' attacks happen constantly now. Stories of the problems of those who have returned without waiting for the official evacuation filter back into the camp. Rumours flourish.

The UNHCR calls for international non-government agencies to tender for various tasks to assist the resettlement. Nee and Phaly discuss what they might do to ensure the safe return of the patients in their care. They type a submission; nobody invites them to submit it but they do. They are not part of an international NGO. They receive no response.

A Canadian agency wins the UNHCR tender for social services for vulnerable returnees. There are limits on their scope to employ a refugee but Thalika decides to apply. He tells me that he has submitted his CV listing his experience and the courses he has taken in Site 2. He has been interviewed.

Thalika's wife has a newborn son, whose life has come at a time of fragile hope. The family is overjoyed when the application succeeds. They will leave the camp ahead of the departure of the first buses. Thalika feels confident. He will need to be if he is to protect his wife, this baby, his other son, his wife's three children of her first marriage and his quadriplegic brother. They face an unknown future somewhere in Battambang Province.

Phaly's son Thero succeeds in finding work with the United Nations Transitional Authority in Phnom Penh. Their operation needs young Cambodians who speak English and who have computer skills.

For the rest of our friends there is no way of imagining how to make a fresh start back in their country.

Ω

The morning set for the official beginning of departures is clear of cloud and blazing with heat. Journalists from around the world flock to Site 2 to record the event. After total silence during the Khmer Rouge era and limited reports of recent sufferings, journalists and camera crews jostle for position. The departure is ideal for film.

I am edgy with resentment at this intense media coverage. I watch it through a lens of petulance. Why now? Why this filming of apparent jubilation while for decades the suffering of the people was scarcely recorded? Whatever they film and write now can never capture the complexity of what is happening.

Young female classical dancers, who will not be on these first buses to return, are dressed in traditional costume, bejewelled, powdered and painted. With a mat for the stage and the sun for stage-lighting they perform the slow and elegant movements of the dance. Musicians play the traditional stringed instruments and percussion. Dignitaries from the United Nations, Thai officials, and representatives of international bodies involved in the planning for this day, watch and listen from a shaded vantage point.

THE BEGINNING OF THE ENDING

The refugees whose names were drawn from the ballot stand in the queue exactly as depicted on the silk-screen banners. They stand in the blazing sun with their babes in arms, their small children and their meagre belongings. Tens of thousands of other Site 2 residents crowd at vantage points and listen.

There are long speeches in English. Very few of the Cambodians understand English. Eventually the buses depart, swirling dust in their wake. The traditional musicians manage to play funeral music. The UN officials and the journalists don't recognise the meaning of what they hear.

$$\Omega$$

Violent incidents with squads of armed bandits, who are almost certainly former soldiers, become more and more common in the camp. Foreigners are evacuated as the bandits approach.

Those who have not departed in the first weeks of repatriation are suffering more intensely now.

In May fire sweeps through the bamboo and thatch huts leaving six thousand people homeless and the MHTH buildings destroyed. Nee is in Thailand, I am in Cambodia. The shelter of Nee's family is burned. 'Run Raksmey, run,' his grandmother calls, holding her arms out to him, and he runs to her through a tunnel of flames. The fire rages unchecked for four hours while bullets, grenades and other live ammunition hidden in huts and administration centres explode without pause. Teenagers are found torching the bamboo and thatch; they confess that masked men paid them to do this.

Nee returns. The MHTH team gathers around him again. In just three days they rebuild the centre.

WRITING FOR RAKSMEY

In June there is a mass demonstration. As soon as the violence turns against foreigners Thai authorities surround Site 2 from the outside, the barang are evacuated and barred from re-entering, the refugees are left to fend for themselves with no delivery of food, water or medical supplies. The Centres for Healing continue caring for vulnerable people trapped inside the camp while Nee maintains radio contact with aid workers in Ta Phraya.

Ω

Site 2 is coming to an end like a candle flame spluttering and drowning in hot wax.

I return from my work in Cambodia. People whom I know are still waiting for their turn. Among this small group of refugees, many are certain that repatriation will mean death. Some prepare for death with Buddhist or Christian rituals. And some say, 'We will burn the buses when they come to take us.'

After Site 2 is completely empty I hear that Thailand bills the United Nations for back rent of this barren piece of land. The thatch and the bamboo rot away. A few years later all that can be found to mark the place is the cement floor of the UNBRO office.

Part II

The Return

14

BACK TO CAMBODIA

There will be protest, there will be hardship, there will be continuing war. There will be joyous family reunions. Some among these thousands will achieve what is hoped; they will have the means to rebuild their lives and to feed their family every day when the 400 days of rice ration comes to a close. Some – many – will be trapped in their poverty, memories, or real and present danger. Or sometimes in all of these things.

From the early days of the return I am criss-crossing Cambodia on behalf of the Australian Overseas Service Bureau (later to be renamed Australian Volunteers International), documenting what is happening, suggesting ways in which Australian volunteers might help.

$$\Omega$$

Phaly and Soeun travel through Battambang to Phnom Penh. By agreement with the UNHCR they are accompanying a group of widows and orphans from KPDR back into Cambodia. I meet them there.

Phaly's widowed mother has a block of land at the end of a dirt road out near Pochentong Airport. Soeun is confident that he can use the repatriation allowance to begin building something there for the orphans, something permanent for these children and for others inside Cambodia who will have the same need. Young Thero, they tell me, is doing well in his work with UNTAC (the United Nations Transitional Authority for Cambodia). They are keen to reach Phnom Penh and to be reunited with family.

Soeun remembers Battambang as he knew it when he was young. He has treasured memories of the river being 'khieu', an intense blue colour. There are popular songs about the bridge and the river, for when Battambang was a thriving university town it symbolised romance. Some still call the river Stung Khieu rather than the official name Stung Sangkae. I watch Soeun letting go of memories as he stands on the bridge looking down. The river water is murky brown. Up-river from Battambang town the Khmer Rouge gouge the riverbed, trading gems to Thai businesses in order to buy weapons.

The restaurant Stung Khieu, with its balconies leaning over the river, the only building on the riverside in the commercial part of town, was once the pride of Battambang. Now, though it still serves some meals, it is a seedy brothel.

There is nothing to keep Soeun and Phaly in Battambang. They look towards Phnom Penh as their future. These friends were already successful adults when forced out of Phnom Penh. I have no doubt at all about their future success in whatever they choose.

While Soeun builds the shelter for the orphans, he plants trees that one day will give shade, and will make a garden. Phaly will find support for a substantial orphanage. Though I will usually be in Battambang rather than in Phnom Penh I will hear news of them from time to time. They will buy more land to expand the orphanage. They will establish a reputation. Phaly will be honoured with international humanitarian awards.

In just a few years my copy of the popular Cambodia Daily will have Thero listed as Business Manager.

Ω

Nee, Monee, Monee's mother Yeay (meaning 'grandmother') and the children wait in the camp until late in the repatriation. Yeay has a married daughter in Sisaphon; her house will be their first destination.

It is the rainy season.

News of their arrival in Sisaphon travels down the line to Battambang. I am staying there in Kevin Malone's house on the north bank of the river; it is a tiny, friendly place, a house he has rented while working in this town. Because Kevin worked on the border and is well remembered, his house is already offering hospitality to Cambodian people who have returned but not found a place where they can live.

Kevin and I decide that as soon as we both have a free day we will travel north to welcome the Meas family; Kevin has a motorbike and is well practised at finding border friends as they arrive. We know that Yeay's daughter lives somewhere close to the river bank on the south edge of Sisaphon town.

The rain is relentless as we set out. When we stop at a small Sisaphon shop close to the river to ask about the Meas family we are sloshing in mud. The river is still rising. We find Yeay and Monee; the women greet me with relief and embarrassment. The shrinking space where they live is crowded with people; houses closest to the river are becoming submerged. In makeshift shelters wet clothing hangs everywhere. It is sordid. These women managed to keep everything clean in the challenges of camp life; keeping clean in this smelly mud where there is no sanitation or water supply is more than they can manage.

The few established houses here are now overcrowded and surrounded by relatives, acquaintances and total strangers squatting all around them in plastic, cardboard and thatch shelters. The neighbourhood is monochrome grey-white and black: mud and brooding skies with sheets of rain. Srey Leak and Raksmey are miserable. They huddle on a plank under a thatched roof. Nee is not with them. He is doing all he can to arrange for sanitation and clean water, anxious about the danger of an outbreak of disease.

There is no joy here. Yeay is glad to see her Sisaphon daughter but doesn't want to stay. Kevin, always hospitable, is offering shelter in his Battambang house.

I meet Nee. He is tired, worried, grubby and longing for the chance to travel south to see his mother. His dark spirit is contagious; it tugs me down towards despondency. Nee tells me the story of the family's arrival.

On their day of departure from the camp the fleet of returnee buses followed behind a heavy truck bringing Australian demountable buildings to Battambang. These are office buildings for the Australian peace keepers. The load was wide and heavy. The road, not too stable at its best, was churned to deep, soft mud in the stretches where the surface broke. On the Thai side of Sisaphon their bus bogged and could not be budged. The returnees and their children waded through mud and rain, dragging their belongings with them. Now they are again under the edge of someone else's house.

We leave them, unsure of what they will do next.

WRITING FOR RAKSMEY

Ω

After a few weeks Nee, Monee, Srey Leak, Raksmey and Yeay respond to Kevin's invitation and join us in Battambang. This gives Nee the opportunity to travel south to Svey Reing, pulled by his longing to be with his mother and sisters and brother after all these years. He returns to Battambang burdened and depressed.

His mother seems frail, different from the way he thought of her during the years of separation. His brother and sisters and new brothers-in-law are poorer than he imagined they would be. He wants to help them: not only out of obligation as eldest son but mostly because he has missed them and feels again his love for them. Counting Monee's family as well as his own there are at least seventeen relatives who hope for his help. His mother-in-law, Yeay, insists that his responsibility is to his wife and children.

Ω

In the close sharing of life in Kevin's little house by the river I begin to understand Yeay.

Raksmey and Yeay sleep on a mat close to me. The little boy has nightmares; Yeay thinks he is dreaming of the fire. Each time he murmurs in distress she folds her arm around him and comforts him. She would give her life for these children.

I recall the memorable rainy afternoon in the camp when I first spent time with Yeay.

Nee, whom I was teaching to drive, bogged the Ute in Site 2 mud and tried to free it using his distant memories of hauling ox carts from soggy ground. The wheels spun and I, as I stood close by, dripped from head to toe with mud.

Yeay was watching. Muttering reprimands at Nee she led me inside, produced a bucket of water and a cloth to sponge off the mud, put all my muddy clothes into the bucket and gave me a dry set of her own clothes. When I sat beside her dressed in her sarong and best white top embroidered with butterflies she was at ease with me, a woman of her own age, an equal.

There was a photo of Yeay's husband, a handsome young man in the uniform worn by officers in Prince Sihanouk's army before the coup of Lon Nol. I was told his story.

He was based in Battambang when the Khmer Rouge occupied the town. The family lived on the south side of the Stung Sangkae. When a message came that a bus would bring Sihanouk's former senior military officers to meet the Prince in Phnom Penh, Sihanouk's men dressed carefully in their best uniforms and prepared for the journey. They were driven to Phnom Ta P'dai, a mountain about an hour from Battambang, and were herded from the bus into a carefully prepared trap and shot dead.

Beneath the pile of bodies was one officer, wounded but not dead. He dragged himself back to Battambang where his family hid him for a time until the Khmer Rouge soldiers found him, pulled him from under a bed, and killed him in front of his wife and children. This officer was someone Yeay knew very, very well. She feared for her children.

Yeay understood that in those dangerous times the south side of the river was thick with Khmer Rouge informers; the north side was a little safer. With her baby boy, Sina, her little girl, Monee, and the rest of her young children, Yeah managed to cross the river in the dusk and shelter in the water-weeds, keeping the children quiet until it was safe to climb out, determined to do all she could to safeguard their lives. In a striking feat of courage she reached the border camp: a step towards safety.

I wonder what it is like for her to be back here in Battambang on the north side of the river once more. I understand her fierce protectiveness. She fought for the survival of her children; she will never give up on this.

$$\Omega$$

Nee knows that he must find work to earn as much money as possible. His mother-in-law hopes that he will take advantage of every opportunity to earn enough to set up a household for her daughter, her son Sina, her two grandchildren and herself. Nee is constantly thinking of the poverty in Svey Reing.

More returnees are settling in Battambang than in any other Province. International Non-Government Organisations committed to assisting in resettlement plan to set up offices here. There was only one INGO when I first came to Battambang; now there are now four. Kevin is recommending Nee to all of them. Nee has a CV detailing his courses and responsibilities in the camp. He speaks English. His skills are needed.

Within a few weeks Nee agrees to develop a program for one INGO, to teach for another and to evaluate for another. None of the work on offer is an exact fit with what he believes is needed for the returnees; he is working to earn money for those he must support. He pushes himself to work as many hours as are offered.

Monee wants to see the family properly housed. At Kevin's house there are mats on the floor for bedding and mosquito nets tied up in every possible direction. In the middle of the night we nudge between other sleepers to reach the single latrine. Monee needs to make a home for her family and Nee's earnings can make this possible.

They walk in the early morning, Nee and Monee together, searching for a block of land for sale. It needs to be close to the town and close to a major road for the sake of security. Further up a side street, even fifty metres further up, would make it more vulnerable to attack by Khmer Rouge. A block is found. Monee strikes a good bargain for it.

The building becomes Monee's project. For the first time she is taking a lead. She holds the family purse, as is the tradition for a wife in a family such as hers. She orders the building materials and oversees the work. Nee provides the money.

During gaps in his arrangements with the big INGOs Nee travels on the roof of the train to Phnom Penh, hoping to link with the university. He still longs to be a healer for his people, and there is more that he needs to learn. He finds no welcome at the university but he keeps trying. From time to time he is able to bring bags of rice to his family further south in Svey Reing.

$$\Omega$$

I am beginning to feel at home in the old, dilapidated Battambang town.

While the day is still cool I walk along Street One, which follows the river. In the gentle first light of morning as the mist rises from the water I see the town as it once was. Even though it is now grimy and battle-scarred, even though I have heard many dark stories of the bloodshed and torture of the recent past and the present time, earlier legends linger. Before the light is too strong the rising sun burnishes the fine old French and Cambodian buildings. I can see what it has been and what it still might be.

Once the light strengthens the present realities are all that there is to see. Beggars cry out for help. They jostle each other: amputees in army uniforms, skinny mothers with skinny babies, toothless old people, and blind people led on a stick or ringing a bell. A tin table with a few stools has been set up as a kerbside café close to the central market-place. The beggars stand behind the customers watching them eating, hoping that left-over food will be passed to them. It usually is; even the comparatively rich diners remember hunger.

On the tower of the market the clock is blank. I am told that when the Khmer Rouge took Battambang in Year Zero the clock stopped. It has not been re-started. It no longer has hands.

15

OUT OF TOWN

As I ride on a motor-dup at the rural edge of town near a rice field flooded for the planting I hear my name called. It is Sok Thim. We both laugh with delight. We share news. 'Imagine us meeting here. You always talked about growing rice. How are your wife and your children? What are you doing with all that knowledge about TB?'

Right now there is no particular place for Thim's knowledge about TB, though he sees many cases untreated in the village where he is living.

We stand with our feet in water and remember Site 2. Thim tells me that Dr Anne Goldfeld is back at Harvard researching infectious diseases. Anne believes that the Site 2 work of establishing protocols for the treatment of TB in conditions of war is useful knowledge for other troubled parts of the world.

The refugee settlements strung along the border were all, during 1981, in the crossfire of a protracted battle. The Vietnamese troops had reached the Thai border. The camps on flat land offered no shelter from shelling; people huddled in a long, deep ditch that had been dug by the Thais to protect their border from invading tanks. The battle continued for weeks. The refugees lived in the ditch: the wounded, the sick, the hungry, the aged, the infants and children. The TB treatment continued, in the ditch, uninterrupted.

Thim worked with Bob Maat as these protocols were developed, then took Bob's place, leading the TB team for all the camps along the border.

Anne has invited Thim to join her in preparing this material for publication.

While my motor-dup driver waits for me in the shade, we stand in the seedbed and we talk of Bob and of Anne.

Bob is still a friend to us both, and we share what we know of him now. With the charismatic Cambodian Buddhist monk, Maha Ghosenanda, he organised and walked the Dharmayatra, the non-violent witness of monks and lay-people, Cambodians and foreigners. Theirs was a pilgrimage through the war zones from the Thai border to Phnom Penh, every step a prayer. CPR organised this vast non-violent cavalcade. I joined with it for a short part of the way. I saw a soldier push through the crowds lining the road, kneel with his AK 47 and rocket launcher in the dust beside him, and ask a water blessing from Maha Ghosenanda.

Anne was among my first friends and colleagues at Site 2; she was director of the American Refugee Committee Hospital near the Centre for Healing. I was there while she supervised the Cambodian medics coping with patients carried into the hospital, smashed and bleeding. The image of the bloody torso of a patient being lowered to the bamboo bench of the hospital, into the hands the Cambodian medics gowned, masked and ready to receive what is still a living young man, stays with me. When I close my eyes I see it and remember horror and pain. Thim and I recall the relentless efforts Anne made as she started the 'ban landmine campaign' in those early days.

Thim shakes his head, putting the past behind, and teasingly invites me to plant while we talk. Catching his mood and his intention I laughingly agree. Thim is a farmer at heart. He knows the smell of the rice fields. The task is to transplant seedlings from the dazzling green seedbed to the flooded fields. He relishes this. I make my first awkward attempts to hold a bundle of wet seedlings in my left hand and, while standing in water, to bend down and plant one seedling at a time in the mud at my feet. This is the bliss of homecoming for Thim, a clumsily performed chore for me. Try as I might I have to keep stopping to stand upright and arch my aching back.

Thim is planting rapidly. 'Had good practice in Khmer Rouge times,' he says. His mind is still on the project he will be doing with Anne. He tells me that it is essential that TB medication is routinely and consistently administered, or stopped altogether lest new strains of drug-resistant TB develop. Bob and the Cambodian medics whom he trained developed a protocol to continue the treatment in a war zone. Daily observed therapy – DOTS – they called it.

We part at sunset. Thim has found a small place to settle his wife and sons. There is no talk of his parents and I do not ask. I must return to Battambang town but we promise to meet again.

$$\Omega$$

It is on Street One that Ky Ka, who worked in the camp with a social-service project for people disabled by landmines or war injuries, skids to a stop on his motorbike and hails me. He is back in Battambang without having accepted UN assistance. This is his town and Battambang Province is his province. He welcomes me to it with gusto.

Ka is travelling to distant villages to see how those who have returned with serious disabilities, those without limbs or without sight, are managing. I am learning whatever I can for the sake of the Australian volunteers.

He urges me, 'You can come with me. You will meet more people if you go with me. There's room on the bike. Look.' He pats the small rectangle of padded cushion behind his seat. 'We will meet …' Ka's attention shifts.

An ox cart loaded with wooden beams is moving along Street One. The rough-cut timber could be a house frame. Sure enough a man, a woman and their small children are perched on top of the load. Their belongings are gripped beside them, packed in striped bags. 'Option B,' we both say.

Ka does what I will see him do time and again. He waves for the cart to stop. 'Where are you hoping to settle? What camp did you come from? How are you managing? Do you need any help?' It is a welcome like the welcome he has offered me.

Ω

I see Ka waiting the next morning at the corner where we agreed to meet: a sturdily built young man, not very tall. His dark hair is straight and cut close to his head; it stands up in bristles. He constantly wears a broad grin, baggy jeans slipping on his hips and a tee-shirt. He smokes a cigarette whenever he is still and sometimes while he rides his motorbike.

Ka instructs me and settles me on the back of the bike. We will not worry about such customs as a woman riding side-saddle, or a woman not touching a man in public. Remote villages are on rough roads; in Ka's judgement safety comes before following tradition. 'Sit on the bike this way … right foot on the small pedal on the right side, left foot on the small pedal on the left side … be careful of the exhaust pipe, it is hot … hold on to me.'

Tracks linking the more distant villages are narrow. When farmers by the trackside greet Ka in a pleased-to-see-you-again tone his return greetings leave them laughing.

Phnom Ta P'dai is about ninety minutes by motorbike from Battambang town. While Ta P'dai is mostly remembered as the mountain where the Khmer Rouge executed the busload of army officers, the foot of the mountain is a close settlement of local village people and their returnee relatives.

There is an old man who squats on his heels in a Cambodian gesture of waiting. He is wearing a faded krama tied around his waist. It reaches to his knees. His bony chest, shoulders and back are bare; he is wrinkled and tanned tough as leather from years of working in the sun. He is at ease. Ka and I squat beside him in the doorway of his bamboo-and-blue-plastic shelter.

Ka's total attention is directed to conversation with this toothless elder who nods towards the flurry of activity inside the hut. His daughter is attending to the household: calming a baby, securing a sarong, lifting and lowering buckets from a shoulder pole. She has been a refugee in Site 2. Now she has a husband and three children.

The young woman presses her palms together and bows before squatting beside us. She knows that living here, so close to landmines, is against the advice of UNHCR. 'Where else would I go?' she asks. 'Our land is here.' She points upwards to a place high on the forbidden mountainside.

Ω

Ka and I detour to Ka's family home. This is a substantial house. The rounded poles that support it have a smooth, shining patina, coming from a time when such great tree trunks were crafted to support houses that would last. The house holds the story of a long-established family. Generation after generation has leaned against those sturdy poles, rubbed them after rain and tied hammocks and mosquito nets to them.

At the top of the ladder is a spacious interior. Many friends and relatives whom I must now meet find shelter here. Ka's wife and young children are living with him in this house where the family has lived for so long. Ka introduces me to his sisters. 'This one has the name of a flower. She is shy to speak. Just smile at her. This one works at the drinks shop down in the town.'

When I meet Ka's mother I know that her formal welcome is on behalf of all. The responsibility she has taken since the execution of her husband and his brothers is unlikely to be handed over easily to a son returning from the border. She will be carefully assessing the daughter-in-law, Ka's wife, whom she did not choose.

Lok, Ka's younger brother, was with him at the border. They are the only members of the Ky family who were in Site 2. It is an easy return. Here among his relatives, Ka sits cross-legged on the polished wooden floor, as is custom. He flicks the ash of his cigarette on to the ground behind him, his conversation a stream of playful repartee.

Ka's father was an important man in Battambang, as was each father's father in the generations before. I imagine them as formal gentlemen, though I cannot begin to imagine Ka as one.

OUT OF TOWN

Ω

The Ky family name is still influential. Ka introduces me to the Assistant Governor of the Province. He is a powerful man, scornful of the fact that the returnees will be issued a rice ration from the UN for 400 days. 'Nobody starves to death in Cambodia,' he says, looking at me reproachfully. 'These are the people who have taken the wrong path.'

The UN presence is strengthening and UNTAC peacekeepers, Australian soldiers among them, have come to live and work in Battambang. Ka takes me to the army compound. A soldier driving out, as we ride in, lowers his car window and shouts 'Ow yu goin? OK luv?'

'No probs,' I say.

Ka lurches to a halt. 'I didn't know you spoke a third language.' He likes the sound of it. I resolve to give him a book of Australian slang; it will appeal to his larrikin streak.

Ω

Ka takes me to a village twelve or thirteen kilometres off the main highway, Highway Five. You can see that it is a less favoured position because the houses along the dirt track have become more and more makeshift, the children more ragged, parasite-bloated bellies and rust-coloured hair of kwashiorkor more common. There is malnutrition. 'Go to the people, listen to the people,' says Ka in a tone that makes fun of his own earnestness. I'm thinking that he needn't try to disguise it. He is soft as marshmallow.

We stop at random: Ka knows nobody here. We squat on our heels in the doorway of a low shelter, joining the family gathered there in a circle of conversation. Pigs are tied up close by; the pig smell is overpowering. Since pigs eat food that people might otherwise eat, and since people here are malnourished, raising pigs is a tempting gamble but an imprudent investment. Raising a piglet to maturity so that it is ready for sale could lift this family beyond barely subsisting. The profit could set up a small business, but the odds are against this happening.

I am here to listen, not to judge. I look at 'the people': old uncles, younger uncles, older aunts. There is a cluster of children gathered to see what is happening. The eldest, a girl of about eight years old, holds a toddler firmly on her hip.

An uncle is saying that treatment for a sick pig is as expensive and remote as treatment for a sick child. If treatment could be found it would drive a family deep into debt. He shakes his head and clicks his tongue, 'Tchk, tchk, tchk.' A child in a neighbouring hut has just this week died of untreated dengue fever. He compares this to the time before the Khmer Rouge, a time when poor people could often hope to have their sickness treated. 'There should be something we can do about this,' he says.

Som Ol has his uncle's pig on a lead and is taking it for a walk. Six years old, he strides out like a man. The uncle nods, 'Perhaps the barang lady would like to take one Cambodian boy back to her country.' The swagger drops away from Som Ol. His lip trembles then he turns his head away from me.

'No, no' I say. 'Som Ol belongs here.'

The aunt calls from her hammock, 'Take Bora, he eats more rice.' Ka joins in the teasing; there is a circle of laughter now.

OUT OF TOWN

As she swings in her hammock the aunt begins to tell a story. She is good at it. Her face is mobile and her eyes flash. Someone was careless in tying the pigs up. Two strayed towards the minefield unnoticed until they were just inside the edge of it. 'Of course each man, woman and child knows the danger of the minefields' she says. The children nod on cue. They watch her, wide-eyed, as the hammock swings to emphasise the importance of this story. 'Nobody, absolutely nobody can go into the minefield to bring back those piglets.' The children again nod as she pauses. The aunt flings out her arms and claps her hands loudly twice. 'Bang. Bang.' The children have been waiting for this climax.

Next comes the lesson. A grown man or woman may slowly bleed to death, or be rescued then taken away for amputations. The children have heard these messages many times. They watch my face. There is a minefield on the other side of their fence. Pigs die quickly if they step on a landmine. So do children.

16

A HOME

With Monee's constant attention her new house is rapidly taking shape.

The poles that support the building are each set in a cement base. They are high enough for me to stand erect where the cooking will be done beneath the house. Wooden steps lead up to the main living area. The walls are timber, the roof is tin, the windows, though without glass, all have metal bars for security. There is an upstairs veranda around the cooler east and north sides. Through the door from the veranda there is one large room with a corner partitioned to make a space for me. The family hopes that I will stay with them for a while.

There is a small shrine. The picture of Yeay's dead husband is on the wall next to the picture of Nee's dead father.

Early one morning before the day is too hot we assemble in the newly built house: Monee, Nee, Yeay, Sina, Srey Leak, Raksmey and me. The monks are coming to chant and perform the ritual to cleanse this home of any bad spirits that might linger.

Following Monee and Yeay's lead I have dressed in the best clothes I can find. Monee is wearing a new som-bpoout of embroidered cloth, the skirt tight enough to accentuate her graceful curves. She has been to the hairdresser and her wavy hair is cut into a very short 1920s

A HOME

bob, a fashion easy for Battambang hairdressers to manage. Nee has bought jewellery for her. Raksmey and his father have white shirts, Srey Leak a frilly dress. Yeay is wearing the white top embroidered with butterflies.

There is a new floor mat unrolled in the middle of the upstairs room. The weave is plastic rather than straw – a small luxury – with a coloured image of Angkor Wat woven into it. Set on the mat are bowls of fruit in gilt containers, incense sticks in holders and gifts of cigarettes for each of the monks who will cleanse the house and burn the incense.

Neighbours sit on the ladders of their own homes to watch and listen. The monks arrive with saffron robes and shaved heads, mount the steps, settle themselves on the mat and begin to chant. The chanting lasts a long time, Raksmey is wriggling, the smell of incense is filling the house. Soft drinks are passed to the monks, Fanta and Sprite. The chanting slows and stops. The monks leave with their gifts.

$$\Omega$$

By mid-afternoon a spell of seemingly unending heat is climaxing with an unexpected thunderstorm. Clouds mount and teeter, blocking the sun, stilling the dogs. Sharp claps of thunder grow louder and closer, the sky splits with lightening, water descends in sheets. It thuds on the new tin roof and streams down the timber walls; precious water caught in buckets in tubs in jugs in dishes.

Neighbours from all along the street join in happy co-operation, forming a chain to bucket water into larger tanks. This morning they were paying good money for dirty river water; the unexpected water from the sky is free. With hair dripping, clothes clinging to bodies, feet bare, the neighbours call greetings to each other. Children dance and squeal their glee, naked in the puddles.

Nee is the first to notice danger. He calls to the children 'Stand back. Stand back,' and pushes them away from the big old kapok tree on the edge of the track. Now everybody notices. The entire root system has broken loose from the soft soil and the tree is standing only because its branches are caught in the new electricity wires. Nee climbs to the swaying tree top, water streaming from him. He swings a hatchet to disentangle the boughs from the wires.

Everybody's attention is on the tree top now.

'The wires might be live.'

'There is never electricity in the afternoon'

'What if there is today?'

Nee continues flailing away with the hatchet from the midst of the gradually descending bed of branches until he stands upright in the mud astride the fallen trunk.

So it is that the Meas family, returnees, politically different, 'the people who took the wrong path', become part of the community of this street.

17

KHMER WAY

In the Meas household Monee is calling Srey Leak and Raksmey to come inside. It is time to stop playing in the street. Darkness will come quickly and the gates must be locked. She calls the dogs too and they come at the sound of her voice. Monee is good with animals.

The day is folding away. At the other end of the street the sun drops in a blaze of vermilion as the noise of children's shouts and laughter, the soundtrack of the day, switches off. The dogs bark protest inside the high fence, then they too settle into quietness.

On the veranda at the top of the stairs I sit on a mat with Nee and Ka; this is the best position to catch any evening breeze that might follow after the heat. At our end of the street a full moon slips up almost unnoticed from behind the coconut palms by the river.

We have spent the day in villages: Ka and I together, Nee for his work with an INGO. These two men were acquaintances in Site 2; here they are developing a friendship. They are drinking beer, adding chunks of ice bought from a peddler who sells from a basket filled with wet sawdust.

Ka is smoking and flicking the ash between the veranda rails. He has learned some Australian slang, 'She'll be right mate', and tries it out with a heavy Cambodian accent. He talks about the young village leader in Doung Kuot who is clearing landmines by hand for neighbourhood women who have no husband to take this risk for them. I'm adding the part about the village leader's wife; she is pregnant with her third child and is both proud of her husband and afraid for him.

The heat gives way to a faint hint of coolness. The fragrance of steamed rice with the pungent smell of fried ginger and fish drifts to the upstairs veranda. There is laughter from the kitchen at the foot of the stairs. Monee has gathered a circle around her as she cooks. She is telling a story about the market, mimicking the characters she met there this morning, entertaining her mother and the children as she piles rice on their plates.

Ka and I are joking together. Nee wants to catch our attention. I'm noticing that these days he has little time for small talk even over a beer. He reaches to a bag on the floor behind him then settles with biro in hand and a notebook balanced on his knee. 'Look,' he says. 'A village is like a basket.' He doodles a sketch across a double page of the book as he talks. 'The basket has been broken and the pieces scattered. The pieces are still there but not everyone can see them.' Ka and I are listening now. 'There has to be a Khmer way of bringing the pieces together,' says Nee.

Ka has been to a community development course in the Philippines. 'Go to the people. Stay with the people. Listen to them. Let them hear each other. Let them plan together what to do. Make sure they know enough and have enough resources to succeed. When it is finished they will say "We did it ourselves".' He laughs at his summary and adds, 'Comrade.'

Nee talks to Ka about MHTH: the experiences, the training courses, what he has learned.

KHMER WAY

'No use thinking of one person at a time now. The pieces needed for restoring life are there in the village. Go to the people, be with the people,' says Ka.

They talk now as if everything is possible. There is no mention of the booming of shells each night, of trucks crammed with the soldiers heading along the road to Palin to do battle with the Khmer Rouge each day, or of the tank always stationed in the centre of town outside Wat Kandal. There is no mention of the humiliation they both experience as 'people who took the wrong path'.

I help Monee to carry the food she has prepared up the stairs to the mat on the veranda: steamed rice in a silvered container, serving dishes of soup, vegetables and fried fish. We eat it with the silent respect that it deserves.

There are sounds of laughter, faint at first but coming closer, from revellers somewhere along the riverside. Long ago, before the troubles, it was the custom on the night of the full moon for young people to be permitted to walk and sing in the street. I watch Ka and Nee; their chance to be care-free on the full moon night was interrupted by the years of forced labour for the Khmer Rouge. Now they click half-full beer glasses together light-heartedly as if eating and drinking in friendship is a familiar experience. 'Mian so!n dtei! piap,' says Ka. We have freedom. Yes. At this moment they taste freedom.

Ω

We look at the villages in a different way: 'The broken basket with the pieces still there,' we say. Something new can be woven.

There are leaders out there. They could re-weave the basket. Not the same as before but, if trust is restored, who knows what it could become. Ka and Nee spend a night of talking, and another, and another. 'Khmer way,' I hear. Night after night I sit with them as they plan. 'Khmer way.'

I watch these two young men together. Their personalities are completely different but in one thing they are the same. Each has deep respect for all life, especially where life is vulnerable; they are always attentive to this. Though I know that both are sceptical about Buddhist practices it seems to me that their hearts are shaped by Buddhism.

I go to a village with Nee. Whichever person he is listening to has his total attention, no matter what else is happening. Every encounter teaches him. 'You have survived. Tell me how you survive.' He tilts towards the person to gather the answer: it is not the way he acts, it is the way he is.

$$\Omega$$

Ka and Nee are thinking about a team.

Two more men are mentioned, Ean and Reth; they could be keen to join in. They're not from Site 2. Ka knows another who was never at the border: Yeth is a vet from the local Department of Agriculture. Ka's sister, Lum Aung, was never at the border either. She would be willing to join if a team was forming.

When I first meet Lum Aung I have the impression of a rather sedate Cambodian woman dressed in an outmoded style that would be better worn by someone older. Lum Aung is probably in her late thirties. When she begins to talk I sense her strength. She talks with passion about women who are poor, women who have been deserted by their husbands and who are neglected by the administration at every level. Who will treat them with dignity?

Lum Aung is sure that it will not be difficult to find good people to form a team; she suggests Bunthan and Sean Lay, who have worked steadily inside Cambodia with the Women's Association. They could be interested.

It is time to put a detailed proposal on paper. I question, listen and write what I hear. It is shared and reshaped, week by week.

18

NOTICING

The United Nations Transitional Authority in Cambodia is assuming its role in Battambang according to the Peace Accords. White four-wheel drives with the blue UN emblem painted on the side are commonplace in Battambang now. They pass each other along Street One and Street Three. They head across the bridges, some travelling north, some travelling south. Each vehicle also has the blue UN flag fluttering from a pole. In the blur of a monsoonal downpour they look like medieval knights jousting. A large house not far from the river is set up as the UNTAC office.

Peacekeepers in their blue berets, some with a small Australian flag sewn to the sleeve of their shirt, are shopping in the market, travelling across the countryside.

On the wall of the UNTAC office is a map of the province with areas shaded in blue, areas shaded in green and areas shaded in red. They represent residential areas, rice fields and minefields. Chillingly the red areas – the mine fields – overlap with the others.

Out in the villages the routines of daily life go on unchanged. Even in the town there are things happening that 'the UN' is not yet noticing.

Ω

NOTICING

Nee and I are heading back from a village to Battambang town; I am on the back of his motorbike. At this time of morning the road is busy. It narrows to the width of the Old Battambang Bridge. Cyclos, bikes, motorbikes and cars jostle into the compressed space.

'Hold on,' he says. At the edge of the bridge Nee's hands tighten on the handle bars, his muscles tense, he weaves and swerves, not pausing in his pace. I shift my weight as the bike tilts. In this tangle of movement nobody is stopping or even slowing. I concentrate on keeping my knees within the width of the bike and my feet above the burn of the exhaust. We fill our lungs with exhaust fumes and dust. Every driver who has a motor horn presses on it as though the sound will carve a pathway through the chaos.

At the edge of my attention is one patch of stillness. Close to the railing of the bridge an elderly man is standing, hands pressed together, bent from the waist in a gesture of deep politeness, a sa-tor. An affluent, middle-aged woman leans from her car. Nee has noticed too. He swerves closer to the car then seizes the opportunity of a break in the traffic to reach the end of the bridge.

'See that?' he says. 'Stay here under the bridge … be careful ... wait for me.' His purple shirt is patched with sweat now.

I don't like being dropped off without explanation, and move to where I can look up at what is happening on the bridge. Spectators are standing around the stationary car. Nee is pushing through the crowd, gesturing with his hands until he reaches the centre of the knot of onlookers where he disappears from my sight. Then the car moves on and he comes back for me.

'What was that about?'

'Didn't you see the gun?'

'Where?'

'The woman was holding the gun at that old man's head. He was pleading with her not to shoot.'

There was no sound of a shot before the car moved on. I don't ask how the threat was resolved.

Noticing is important: looking and listening.

Ω

My own daily life rubs against the lives of my Cambodian neighbours. Everywhere I see crutches, rough-hewn prostheses and wheelchairs. A bicycle passes and I notice that the rider has only one leg. I often see women and men with so little of the stumps of legs left that it is impossible to fit prostheses.

A young man I greet each day has literally no stumps at all. He sits on a skateboard and pushes himself along with his hands on the ground as someone his age in Australia would push through the water while sitting on a surfboard. He is both athletic and enthusiastic. He propels himself between bikes and tools, learning the trade of motorbike repair and working to build up a small business. Everywhere there is courage. Often there is humour.

A woman in the sewing section of the market offers to mend a small rip that she notices in the skirt I am wearing. I move closer to her sewing machine so that she can position the damaged fabric under the needle, clip it down, and stitch it. She laughs infectiously as she threatens to charge me 'two dol-lars' for a minute of work and companionship, but will only accept two hundred Cambodian riel, the equivalent of a few cents.

As I sit side by side with Nee waiting near the market a three-legged cat nuzzles against us. This pathetic creature must have endured all kinds of infections after losing a limb in the midst of squalor. It has survived. I look at Nee and think of his survival, and the survival of the double amputee on the skateboard, and the survival of the laughter of the woman in the market. I blink away tears that have been threatening for a long time. I turn my head so that Nee doesn't notice. I'm not ready to talk about this.

Ω

By the end of '92 Nee and Ka have refined their vision. It is written down. We have sent it through Phnom Penh to the Overseas Service Bureau in Melbourne. I'm invited to discuss it in Australia: there may be some funds available for supporting village communities to recover from the tragedies of these years. Australian volunteers might be involved.

I believe in the pattern of what could be done. It is as Ka and Nee envisaged. A small team of Cambodians could work together with village people. They would listen to the hopes of the women and the men, understand the tensions of the ongoing conflict, try to build trust and to nurture leadership.

The Overseas Service Bureau is a flexible Australian NGO. Though set up to recruit, prepare, place and support volunteers it is willing in this case to partner a project that may win Australian oversees aid funding. The workers at OSB know how to frame the application to match the criteria. Eventually a project is put forward as 'discovering, fostering and helping to create activities which bring unity and reconciliation'. It sounds grand but it will boil down to actions that are simple and grounded. I am glad of that.

19

ELECTION YEAR

There is a narrow cement and brick house, an unusual Chinese-style house, built flat on the ground. Ka and Nee have recommended renting it as a base for the new team to meet. The men and women have gathered one by one. Now we are together. It is the beginning of the election year.

Moira O'Leary and Mal Simmons, two Australian volunteers, have come to offer training and support. Soon we understand that they are offering to share the whole of their daily lives.

We sit in a circle on the floor in this rented space. There are decisions to be made. We don't know each other well yet but certain things must be arranged immediately and there is money from Australia, a small budget to be spent wisely. The men and women sitting on a floor mat in a circle understand the practical preparations needed.

First, motorbikes. They agree to purchase five, then eventually a further five motorbikes so that each person on the team will be able to travel to the villages. Ka says, 'Look. They are not expensive bikes. They are ordinary, not much power. The bandits will des-pise them.' He emphasises the word 'despise'; he would quite like to be driving a much more powerful bike but it fits neither the budget nor the vision.

Someone says, 'We will need to hear each other's story.' Two voices together say, 'Why?' I look at the faces around the circle. Five women and five men. They are of the generation that was just reaching young adulthood when the Khmer Rouge seized power in '75. This is what they have in common. During the civil war that followed the Khmer Rouge time they were on different sides, either by choice or by circumstances. They will not sit on this mat and talk about it, at least not now. 'Okay', I think. 'Let it be.' People in every village have this same tension. So do people in many families. We will stay with the practical choices that must be made.

They choose a radio transmitter linked to the UNTAC network. Each person on the team will be responsible for a two-way hand-held radio. It is sensible precaution to tune to regular security warnings and to warn one another of danger.

They decide that it is safer for their group to be known by a foreign name. They choose to use the name of OSB for the Australian Overseas Service Bureau. The call sign for their 'office' becomes Oscar Bravo Base. For individual identification on the two-way field radios it is Oscar Bravo One or Two or Three: a number to match the number on the motorbike.

While we are talking, while we are eating, even while we are sleeping we can hear the announcements. 'Attention all stations there will be a controlled explosion in Bay Dum Run district at fifteen hours. Repeat there will be a controlled explosion in Bay Dum Run district at fifteen hours. Over.'

When the bikes are out in the villages there is always someone rostered to stay at the base in case one of the team calls on the radio for help or needs to be warned of danger.

$$\Omega$$

WRITING FOR RAKSMEY

On an unusually hot February day at the Meas family home I am the first in the household to awaken, at 5 in the morning. I hear the sounds of sleep: the breathing, the turning, the mutter of words, the sighs coming from under the army-green sleeping nets crammed along the veranda. Last night was stifling and we all moved our nets outside to find more air: Yeay with the two children under the net with her, Monee's brother Sina just reaching adulthood and with a net to himself, Monee and Nee sharing a larger net. I am furthest from the ladder, the most protected, with a net and mat of my own.

I adjust a sarong and tee-shirt and feel my way in bare feet across the veranda boards, stooping beneath the ropes that support the nets. At the foot of the steps I slip my feet into sandals, pat the dogs, squeeze through the gate and latch it again. I'm heading around the corner to Wat Sampeu; the head monk with his community of novices is always glad to welcome me and lead me to a quiet place on an upstairs balcony. He is happy to be able to say to his novices 'See, even the barang prays early in the morning.' When all is said and done, these first quiet hours are the best thing that I can do in preparation for the coming day.

My attentiveness moves from seeking God, whose silence is complete, to thoughts of the day ahead.

The first eight villages we will work with have been chosen: the criteria is that they are very poor indeed, that no NGO is working with them, that they are willing to work together as returnees and locals and as members of different factions to solve common problems. They are already hoping that someone from our team will come today with news.

The last star is fading. Behind the coconut palms a fine line of vibrant pink expands upwards from the horizon. The chanting of the monks in a Wat a few hundred meters to the north is joined by the sound of chanting on cassette tape from our Wat; our novices are slow-starters. I see a candle lit for morning in a bamboo shack across the road from where I sit. Roosters crow. The family with the candle tunes a radio to the news in Khmer. In Siem Reap Khmer Rouge attackers have managed to hold the town for a few days.

Today is the day that the Dharmayatra of Maha Ghosenanda and Bob Maat will set out from Siem Reap to walk the dangerous Highway Six to Phnom Penh, every step a prayer. Their walk always begins by dawn; surely they are already walking. Every step a prayer.

$$\Omega$$

In March Khmer Rouge attacks become so frequent that for a time we postpone visits to villages. It is too dangerous to move far from the town. Nee warns me that it is not safe to leave the house before sunrise, and I follow his advice.

There is a regular briefing at the UNTAC compound. Australian peacekeepers have responsibility for communicating warnings of potential attacks. I accept that it is my responsibility to attend meetings. Ka and Nee clown about this.

'Here she comes fresh from the briefing. Roll the cameras. Get her into focus.' They pass an imaginary hand-held microphone and somebody zooms with an imaginary camera. The recently founded Battambang TV channel operates with one hand-held microphone passed from interviewer to interviewee. Our crew have the technique copied exactly.

'Tell us where the UNTAC say the Khmer Rouge are. Spean? Really! And where are they expected to attack next? Really.' Everyone is hooting with laughter and applauding. Battles are certainly being fought. Most of these locals know precisely where and why. They warn me of danger when they know of danger. I follow their warnings unreservedly.

Cambodians and foreigners all agree about the serious risk on election day. The Khmer Rouge has threatened to shell the polling booths. The organisation has pulled away from the Accords they signed in Paris. Most of their troops have refused to disarm. They will not be part of the election. They will carry out their threat.

Ω

For a week in March the UN sponsors a National Women's Summit to prepare women leaders for the election to be held in May. The five women from the team travel by 'taxi' down the risky road to Phnom Penh to attend.

At the end of the week they return exhausted and enthused: Sean Lay, Bunthan, Lum Aung, Sokaty and Chenda. We are gathered in the 'office' waiting to greet them. They each pour a few dippers of water over face, head, arms and feet to rinse off dust and sweat; they eat the fruit we have prepared for them. More than anything else they need to tell us what they have learned.

'In the new Cambodia women will be important.'

'Women form sixty-three per-cent of the population; women plus dependent children form seventy-five percent.'

'We will participate at all levels of policy including drafting the new Constitutions of Cambodia.' They represent the three factions vying for election: two of them support CPP, two support BLDP and one, Lum Aung, supports FUNCINPEC.

ELECTION YEAR

The next day FUNCINPEC calls an afternoon election rally in the Battambang stadium and, galvanised as she is by the conversations she has shared, Lum Aung stands up in the crowd and makes a spontaneous speech about women and their role as peacemakers. She is amazed at the words coming from her mouth. So are those who listen.

As the rally ends Lum Aung is passed a message that what she has just done puts her life in danger. There would certainly be spies in the crowd. She is a marked woman. She should not go to her home but should find somewhere to hide. Her elation evaporates; replaced by fear. Who can help her to hide? It should be somebody on the team who is definitely not FUNCINPEC. Nee? Yes, Nee is not FUNCINPEC and he has the keys of the team's house. The cement wall and bars on the glassless windows mean that this house is a reasonably secure refuge.

The entire team is ready to protect Lum Aung although only her brother shares her support of FUNCINPEC. The team members urge her to sleep in the shelter of the 'office' until the elections are over. Women on the team offer to take turns to stay with her to keep her company and ensure that she is never alone. We will keep the two-way radio on through the night and the men will be 'on call' should we need to summon them to the office.

Each night two or three women are with Lum Aung in this strong house. Most nights I stay with them. We confide hopes and fears but are never too earnest. We paint fingernails and toenails, cream our faces and hands and give each other traditional massage. Cambodian traditional massage is not gentle and as the elder I am the recipient of most of it. I sleep deeply on a straw mat on the tiled floor.

From time to time there is a radio check from one of the men on the team.

'Oscar Bravo Base this is Oscar Bravo Three ... over.'
'Oscar Bravo Three copy ... over.'
'Oscar Bravo Base what is your situation ... over.'
'Situation normal ... Oscar Bravo Base over and out.'

All who dare to be politically active know that they risk their lives no matter which party they belong to. Fury against FUNCINPEC is particularly fierce, for this is the party of greatest threat to the power of Hun Sen's CPP. During this election campaign 114 potential candidates and close supporters are killed in various parts of Cambodia. There are fifty-eight victims of politically motivated murder in Battambang Province. Lum Aung is not one of them.

Ω

Election day dawns with a clear blue sky: a perfect May morning. I sit in the early sunshine on the front steps of the Meas family house catching the frisson of excitement among the neighbours. People along the street are determined to vote but prudently take risks into account. If a polling booth is attacked, as is feared, one parent needs to survive; nobody wants children to be orphaned for the sake of democracy.

Nee and Monee are enrolled and are keen to vote but have planned for one to stay with the children while the other goes to the booth.

Voters have been queuing at the booths since first light. It is said that distant hills were dotted before dawn with the lights of those making their way towards the town. The process has been orderly. Neighbours return from the polling booths excited. They have voted, their fingers are marked with indelible ink.

The Australian TV crew who filmed Thalika after the bandit attack in Site 2, and again when his family first returned to Battambang

Province, trace me from Melbourne to Battambang to arrange to film him on Election Day. Thalika is still working with the INGO that recruited him in the camp. He tells me that he is willing to be interviewed once more.

After the filming the Australians return to thank me. They are pleased with their footage. Thalika answered their questions with his usual clarity

'Why did you go to the border?'

'Because of the shelling.'

'What problems do you have now?'

'Shells are falling close to us.' The Australian cameraman framed Thalika walking towards the polling booth after his interview. This shot clinched their story: a shell fell nearby.

$$\Omega$$

While we wait for the counting of results we return to routine. Each morning two of us are rostered for some housekeeping chores before the work of the day begins. Lum Aung and I are mopping the floor when she says 'I have a problem.' We lean on our mops. 'I have to make a decision and have only a very short time to make up my mind.' She is asking me to listen. We prop our mops against the wall and sit together on the floor.

Prince Ranariddh, the leader of the royalist FUNCINPEC party, has contacted Lum Aung through the UNTAC communication channels. FUNCINPEC have won enough Battambang seats for a place in parliament to be offered to her. She has one day … today … to decide whether to accept.

The other four Cambodian women arrive ready for work. They sit close to Lum Aung on the tiled floor, talking softly in Khmer. 'We are saying to Lum Aung that if she says "No" there will not be an offer to another woman.'

Lum Aung goes home to spend the morning with her family and to come back in the afternoon. We buy Fanta and Sprite from the market to prepare a small party. Lum Aung returns with a shoulder bag packed: folded sarongs, toothbrush, toothpaste, face cream.

Before nightfall an UNTAC helicopter collects Lum Aung to take her to Phnom Penh. She enters a capital taut with anxiety. Prince Ranariddh, a son of Norodom Sihanouk, has gained the majority of votes. FUNCINPEC gained 58 seats, the CPP 51 and BLDP 10. The Cambodian People's Party of Hun Sen controls the army and refuses to concede defeat. A breakaway group of CPP candidates seizes control in six provinces. Their leaders, Prince Chakrapong and Sin Song, announce that they have seceded from the rest of the country. They are supported by military. Cambodia is once more in danger of widespread carnage.

We listen to the radio for every fragment of news, worried for the country and particularly for Lum Aung. Norodom Sihanouk takes the role of peacemaker. CPP, Hun Sen's party, is in control of the army, the police and all institutions of the nation down to village level. Sihanouk suggests a coalition with ministries shared between CPP and FUNCINPEC. There would be two prime ministers.

Lum Aung accepts responsibility in a ministry. There are five women and 115 men in this Constituent Assembly. Their major task is to approve a Constitution for Cambodia, as was foreshadowed in the Peace Accords.

ELECTION YEAR

Ω

Whenever I am in Phnom Penh I spend time with Lum Aung. She still talks of her pity for women and children who are destitute in the villages, saying that since she has no husband or children she is free to give her whole energy to shaping decisions that will help them.

Her sheltered life in Battambang has not prepared her for the huge responsibilities of her new role. Most members of this government lack the education that they need for the task before them; they are learning as they work. Lum Aung is adamant that if she has something to say she will hold her hand up until she is heard.

As she finishes telling me these things she presses her lips together and nods. I never doubt her determination. 'When I am angry, when I have an opinion and need to share it, I can speak faster.'

Ω

Monee is pregnant. She craves durian fruit. I abhor the smell of it but Monee is dear to me so I carry home durian from Phasar Nhat and do whatever else might express my care.

Now that we are together in Battambang I can admire Monee's strength. Here in her own home she takes the lead. I watch her sitting in a circle of Cambodian friends and relatives telling stories. The tight knot of women and men around her are held in rapt attention; she uses her face and her body and her voice to mimic each character in her story. The shy, young wife has disappeared.

Her day always begins early. She wakes with the soft dawn light filtering through her mosquito net, walks quietly to the family shrine and lights the incense to honour the ancestors. It is a familiar and necessary ritual. At the side of the shrine are the fading black-and-white photos of her father and Nee's father as well as a small coloured snapshot wedged between the wallboards of the house. This is the one keepsake of her wedding: there she is, kneeling beside Nee in the Site 2 ceremony. Both look absurdly stiff in hired clothing of bright silks.

Good smells waft from Monee's ground floor kitchen under the living area of the house: onion, garlic, chilli, and constantly steaming white rice. I watch to learn her recipes. 'How long should I cook this Monee?'

The answer is always the same. 'Until it has the good smell.' Everything is to be sniffed.

We are talking women's talk. 'Why do most Cambodian women I know not sit down with the family and eat after they have cooked the meal?' She convinces me that it is more enjoyable for a woman to relax with her meal before or after the family, when there is nothing to do. 'Nothing at all except to delight in the food.' While everyone else is eating there is always rice to serve on to their plates and serving dishes of food to refill. I begin to understand when I share the laughter and gossip around the cooking and eating in the kitchen.

Monee sings popular Khmer songs with a sweet and powerful voice. When American pop music begins to be sold on cassette in Battambang, she sings in English

> Wherever you go, whatever you do,
> I will be right here waiting for you,
> Whatever it takes,
> Oh how my heart breaks,
> I will be right here waiting for you.

I worry about this. She has had enough heartbreak. She tells me she means it; her husband is often out in the villages and she will wait. She begins to speak more and more English.

When her sleep is troubled with nightmares, as the sleep of those who have seen too much often is, Monee rides her bike to a particular Wat where there is a monk with a reputation as a healer. He gives her the ceremony of water cleansing so that she can put the terror of the night behind her and face the day.

$$\Omega$$

Monee's baby is born in the new maternity clinic on Street One in Battambang. She and her husband talk about this as a small luxury, a chance to experience something different. Monee stays in the clinic only long enough for us to gather around the bed and view the little boy. This child with dark curling hair, fragile fingers and pale skin is contented. He returns home with his mother so that Yeay can light the traditional fire, rub with traditional herbs and do all else that is needed. The baby remains placid. Though I live in his parents' house in this year of 1993, he is three weeks old before I ever hear him cry. Life pleases him.

At first his parents think they might name him Somnahng, meaning 'lucky'. They hold to hope because, after more than twenty years of wars and atrocities, he is born while the radio is playing the debate on the new Constitution of Cambodia. Only a month previously Norodom Sihanouk was re-enthroned as king. It seems that peace has arrived and that when this little one begins school most of the children in his class will be called Somnahng.

Before Monee and Nee are firm in their choice of the name the Khmer Rouge army closes in on Battambang once more. The civil war is not over. Somnahng is not the right name for this child. He is named 'the one who takes care': Reaksa. The name suits him from the beginning. 'Be careful to roll the "R".' Reaksa.

A friend from Australia comes to visit. We take him to picnic at the ruins of an ancient temple near the river. He gives us a photo of the Meas family sitting among the rubble of rocks. Yeay is looking out, away from the group, frowning a little. The two small children are huddled against their father, the baby a newborn bundle in his arms. I look again and again at Monee. Her face is cupped in her hands; she seems pensive. I see this look often when she sits quietly with her memories.

Ω

The night is late. We hear movement downstairs in the darkness even though the dogs have not barked. 'Shh,' says Nee, and he moves quietly to the corner of the balcony, where it is possible to see an intruder below without being seen. He gestures to us with his hand behind his back. Caution. Sina moves to stand beside his brother-in-law. In his hand is a gun.

Nee turns his head towards the family and mouths 'Get down low away from the windows.' Yeay has her arms around the three children as they lie on the floor. Monee stays low but slithers flat across the floor boards and lights incense at the shrine of the elders. Sina fires one shot to the sky. This is enough. I imagine dark shadows slinking away.

When Nee is sure that the danger has passed we go downstairs. The dogs lie dead, poisoned. Monee is inconsolable. The bandits have taken a large, blue plastic water tub and my green Chinese pushbike with the brand name 'Peasant' in English. Nothing of great value was there to be stolen. Nee has been totally attentive to his responsibility to protect us all.

A week later, during the UNTAC drive to rid Cambodia of all weapons, Nee hands in the gun so that it will be crushed into scrap metal.

$$\Omega$$

The Khmer Rouge force is advancing on Battambang town once more and has already shelled the bridge. I sit on the grass at 'the field of kick-the-ball' not far from the river, watching as Srey Leak and Raksmey play with their father. Raksmey has changed from a toddler to an independent little boy; he has his opinions and plays with his sister on his own terms now.

Nee is sitting on a patch of ground striped with the late-afternoon rays of the sun. Leak and Smey take turns to come up close behind their father's back. He lifts them one by one in the air; they somersault, shrieking with delight, before Nee guides them carefully around and down until they stand on their feet facing him. They jostle for another turn. Nee knows that back at the house a pushcart is packed and ready. If the Khmer Rouge take Battambang in the next few days, as expected, he will be on the road again, this time with a young baby boy, two small children, a wife and a mother-in-law.

There is nothing I can do to change this and so try to share these moments of joy.

20

ANSANG SOK, SPEAN, CHROY AMPOR, WAT KUNDUNG

The frontline of battle is pushed back towards Palin once more; it is safe to work in the villages and stay there for four or five nights at a time. It is wet season in Battambang Province, the paddy fields are soft and warm, the seedbeds dazzle with luminous green.

I am in the riverside village of Ansang Sok with half of our team. We are not bringing aid, not even projects. The Cambodian women and men of the team are listening to the stories, watching the life here, gaining trust, sharing what they have of daily rice and of time while the people of the village also share with them. They are learning how the people survive, and affirming this. They listen carefully to the ideas of local men and women who have dreams for a future.

They try to enlist a cluster of villagers to choose a leader for a project to repair battered old boats. But the village people do not yet know who to trust. They still struggle to survive individually in any way they can. There will need to be months of building trust, of encouraging and educating local people. This needs careful building of foundations. 'Step by step,' the team say as they realise this.

There is no rice grown here. Before the Khmer Rouge it was a village of jute crops but the jute factory is long gone and families survive on the fish they can catch in the Sangkie. There are some fruit trees but no vegetable patches. The village is inundated with floodwater at least twice a year. It is inundated now, literally awash with none-too-clean mud.

While the women and men of our team fan out through the village to listen to the people I stay beside them, gradually learning the basic skills for living here. I need to master the dexterity of sluicing my muddy feet against the plank of wood set at the foot of the house-ladder. I should elegantly scrape mud from my right foot with my left and my left foot with my right while standing erect, holding a dipper and pouring a steady stream of water down on to my feet. Instead of this effective routine that every child of two has learned, I stoop down and fuss with my hands, rubbing at each bare, mud-clogged foot. 'You are like a duck,' they say. But fondly, as they say it to a child.

It is well beyond my skill to walk steadily upright in the deep slime, though the child selling vegetables does it with the tray balanced on her head. The rice field is the toilet. 'Do you need to pass urine or do you need to pass stool? Go further.'

People talk one on one with the team. They talk in their families and gradually in their neighbourhoods of the challenges of their own daily survival. They reflect on the long ago time when this was a thriving, jute-producing village. What is holding them back from developing again?

We are welcomed to stay in the house of the village leader. We sleep in a line on the floor like sardines in a can. I first met the village leader's wife five months ago on the day she gave birth to their youngest. He is now a charming baby who gurgles with delight when he sees me. The other children are more tentative in their greeting.

I understand ... the routine way of disciplining children here is 'Be good or the barang will eat you.'

Ω

Touern and I set out on the motorbike towards Bay Damran in the late afternoon. Touern has been selected to fill a space on the team. I knew her in Site 2; she is a country woman born in a remote village. When the Khmer Rouge took over in '75 she would have been a young girl with eyes that spoke, dusky skin, and crooked teeth. Her eyes still speak, she is comfortable in her skin and her smile is memorable. She has struggled in poverty and grown in wisdom in the decades since that time.

When I met her in Site 2, Touern was working for the Women's Affairs Association while studying counselling and social work. She was full of hope and energy even then. After the border the only work she could find was cleaning offices. With the income from this she supported four young children and a husband who rarely worked.

She slips into community development in the villages as though she was born for this. Touern is unrelentingly cheerful. This is her instinct, not her doing her job.

It is harvest time in Bay Damran. As we arrive a line of villagers has already assembled to walk to the distant rice field, ready to begin harvesting at dawn. They notice our arrival and have begun to learn that the coming of a foreigner, even one on the back of a motorbike, might signal a handout. They turn from their track through the long shadows and swarm around us as we dismount; understandably they never miss an opportunity to gain the protection of a rich patron. 'We are hungry,' they say. Touern grins. 'And what would you do if we did not come right now?' she asks. They look at her. Nobody speaks. 'I suppose you would fall down on the ground dead,' she says and, without a pause after saying this, without another word, she tumbles down, stretched full-length on the ground. The watchers laugh in delight, pick up their krama-packed bundles and head back down the track through the long shadows.

$$\Omega$$

The three-and-a-half kilometre walk to Chroy Ampor is never as straightforward as it sounds. There is no road. We balance on ridges at the border of rice fields. Six or seven times we must wade through waist-deep water, sometimes for twenty or thirty metres at a time. I am learning to keep my feet under me where they belong, but cannot be relied upon to always succeed. After a few slithering entries and exits to the deep, Ean and the CPP-appointed village leader from nearby Spean each offer me a forearm to clutch as they charge manfully ahead, having done something so uncultured as allowing a woman to touch them in public.

We are soaked from armpits down. My krama is wound around my head. The village leader from Spean is steadying me with his right hand. His left arm is raised above his head, holding his precious AK-47 aloft to keep it dry.

Chroy Ampor is infinitely more miserable than Ansang Sok or Spean, but there are fine people in the village. Ean asks me to take the ever-present, ever-watching Spean village leader for a walk so that the natural leaders of Chroy Ampor can share with the team their own plans for their own village. I should make sure that the walk takes as long as possible.

We follow a muddy path to a stream, the leader from Spean and I. The only way to cross is to balance on a log. It is shining with rain water. The leader is enjoying his role as protector and guide, demonstrating what we should do. He will go first with his gun across his shoulder, edging sideways with his bare feet curved around the log. I will place one hand on each of his shoulders and, steadied by him, slither my own bare feet across the log. We are half-way when he loses balance, splashes to the water and is submerged, AK-47 and all. I slither astride the log, hesitate, then splash down into the water beside him. He need not lose face and this will prolong the time for the Chroy Amphor group to do their planning. We drag ourselves out, clean ourselves up and return to the village by a longer, safer route.

Without hesitation and with much drama, the man from Spean tells the story of how he has bravely rescued me from the water. He laughs uproariously and tells it again and again and again.

Ω

It is evening in the dry season. We are back in Chroy Ampor. Almost our entire OSB team is here, as the people of the village need to celebrate. They have built a road linking their village to Spean; it is completed just before the wet season begins again. This year when the waters rise they will be able to bring their sick people to a clinic and the older girls and boys will walk the three-and-a-half kilometres each way to school. Goods will be brought in and out of the village. It is a fine, high, hand-compacted road, and they are proud.

We celebrate. Everybody in the village is here.

ANSANG SOK, SPEAN, CHROY AMPOR, WAT KUNDUNG

A blue tarpaulin is rolled out at the side of the fire; we would call it a campfire in Australia. Music from a battery-operated cassette player is amplified and we are invited and urged onto the dance floor, eating sweetened black rice and dancing on the blue tarp until the sun rises.

'Go to the people. Listen to the people. Help them to hear one another. Support them to act together. When it is done they will say, "We did it ourselves."'

$$\Omega$$

Natural leaders from many of the villages are ready to come to Battambang to learn together. The rented cement house is no longer adequate.

It is traditional for the Buddhist temples here to have a salla, a teaching-house for poor village people. We negotiate with the Battambang department of religious affairs to rebuild an abandoned salla in the grounds of a local Wat. The monks agree and a contract is signed. Mal is an engineer; he can design something suitable, while the rest of us clear the site.

The salla in Wat Kundung is restored as a simple tiled-roof building with its original brick walls to a metre in height, then with wooden lattice walls to allow breeze to blow through. The team and the people who come from the villages can work together here. This new salla is viewed with pride by the Wat Kundung villagers; it is reached by taking a gravel track between ever-flowering old frangipani trees. We relish their perfume and plant some scarlet-coloured bougainvillea.

Ω

Reth, a woman living in the village of Wat Kundung, has a one-room house that she built with her Option B house frame. She offers it for rent. She wants to move to her mother's house which is beside it and the rent money will help her to care for her children while her husband is at war. I rent the house and make it my home.

There are no fences here. 'Our neighbour is our fence', people say, watching out for each other. Reth and other women neighbours squat beside me as I learn to cook my food in my terracotta cooking pot over a charcoal fire. We talk. They surround me in my daily life, often strolling past as I take a dipper shower clad in a wet sarong, standing on a plank above the mud at my open-air clay water pot, as is custom here. My neighbours ensure that my door at the top of my stairs is securely locked at night. Years later I will understand the steps they have taken to be sure that I am safe.

Ω

Our team in the new centre in Wat Kundung is growing in confidence. It is registered with a Khmer name: Krom Akphiwat Phum. There is a logo, a circle of women and men with hands clasped. Local leaders out in the villages understand that the name means that this group will support the development of village community in every way.

Ω

ANSANG SOK, SPEAN, CHROY AMPOR, WAT KUNDUNG

When UNDP representatives from many countries plan a conference in Phnom Penh they invite Krom Akphiwat Phum to bring some of the team and some local leaders from the villages to contribute. It is a warm evening in mid-March when we gather in Phnom Penh to sleep on the floor of the OSB office, readying ourselves for the conference next day. The organisers have prepared a folder for each of us and there is a sense of occasion.

A leader from the village of Kampong Ko, a name that translates as 'cow paddock', is particularly delighted that the conference booklet gives background information about each village represented. 'I can read and write,' he tells me with pride. I wake in the night to see a pinpoint of light halfway along the dark row of sleepers. The man from Kampong Ko has a flashlight held above his conference folder. He is soundlessly mouthing words while the rest of us sleep.

The conference is held in the grandest venue in Phnom Penh; most participants are wearing suit and tie. In mid-afternoon, when I have become convinced that we are invited simply as observers, there is an invitation for comments from the floor. The man from Kampong Ko raises his hand and stands. 'I am from Kampong Ko.' This is said with great dignity as he stands in rubber sandals, working trousers and faded shirt. 'I can read. You say that Kampong Ko is developing a duck project and a rice barn. Yes, we have a duck project and a rice barn. But really we are developing people. That's what we do. We develop people.'

21

FACING REALITY

The Australian Justice Michael Kirby is appointed as the Special Representative of the Secretary-General of the United Nations for Human Rights in Cambodia. He quickly sums up the situation that faces him: 'In the absence of cantonment the country continued to be rife with heavy weaponry … Armed gangs, petty gunmen, common criminals and off-duty police all freely [commit] murders and other acts of violence.'

When he visits Battambang Michael hears that Australians are working with a Cambodian team. He greets me with interest and I invite him to share breakfast at the salla. We often sit in a circle on the mat sharing something to eat and some hot glasses of tea before the day's work begins; Michael agrees to join us there though he knows that the occasion will be very simple. The women of the team order noodles from the breakfast shop and bring fruit from the market. Since we have no chairs in our circle they stack cushions for our guest to be seated comfortably with the wall as a backrest. Michael enters graciously into the occasion.

The conversation is lively; it leads to the subject of impunity. When Michael wonders whether the Krom team worries that crime is not punished the talk becomes even livelier. Out in the villages we have seen countless examples of unpunished crime. There are times when one or other person on the team has helped good people of the village to bring wrongdoers to face the law. Some on the team argue that 'rule of law' is more important than rice: an amazing opinion from those who have suffered starvation.

'And what about the Khmer Rouge? Will you remember what they have done?' Justice Kirby asks. There is a slight pause before Ka speaks. 'Mr Kirby, I will never forget what they have done. I saw them stand my father and my uncles in a line and kill them. I will never forget.' There is a longer pause. 'If I was to do something about it I would take a gun and not stop shooting until nobody was left standing.'

Justice Kirby knows, as this simple group sitting in a circle on the floor knows, that the 'Khmer Rouge Tribunal', as it is starting to take shape in Cambodia, will be far from the International Tribunal preferred by the United Nations High Commission for Human Rights. We sit in our circle silent before this major dilemma of impunity.

Ω

The Khmer Rouge troops are advancing on Battambang once more. Ka asks, 'What did you do during the shelling last night?' I admit that the attack did not wake me, but return to the Meas household for a brief time, as I promised to do whenever Battambang is being shelled. And I faithfully attend UNTAC Security Briefings in case there is information that the Krom Akphiwat Phum team should know.

Ω

The young Australian soldier in charge of the briefing is sharing information: the train from Phnom Penh to Battambang will be attacked by the Khmer Rouge as it passes through Moung district.

'Is the source credible? Is it reliable?'

There is a high degree of credibility and a reasonable degree of reliability.

'What can be done?'

A report will be filed but the train cannot be cancelled; UNTAC is not responsible for doing that. UN personnel and UN supplies will not be on this train.

Today there is no phone connection between Battambang and Phnom Penh. Tomorrow the train will have Cambodians on the roof and sitting free of charge in front of the engine. It is always like that.

I have no authority and no way to connect with those who have the authority to protect the Cambodians. They will not be warned of danger as they board the train in Phnom Penh. I stay behind after the meeting believing that something can be done, wanting to talk about it. The Australian soldier has a clear line of responsibility. He will file a report meticulously; I can trust in that. But he is not the one to make decisions; he has no more authority than I do. It is as if the ground is disappearing from under my feet.

At the doorway of the demountable office I miss the first of the three steps and fall. In the night I lie sleepless on my mat. I have never before felt so helpless.

The next day I am rostered as the one to 'stand by' the radio. Some of the team are working in villages in Moung district.

'Oscar Bravo Base there are injured people and bodies along the railway line over.'

'Injured people are crawling on hands and knees to find help. Over.'

FACING REALITY

Help is a long way away from the railway line.

The team do what they can. We check local estimates of casualties. There are more than twenty people dead and almost one hundred injured. In helplessness and rage I write to the Australian Ambassador in Phnom Penh. It takes time for the letter to reach him and time for his reply to reach me. Though there has been no media report of the attack he does not dispute what I am saying. He has taken time to check with authorities.

He acknowledges the facts and the tragedy of it. 'Every life is equally precious.'

Ω

One night, as we are about to leave the salla, there is a radio message from Nee and Soeuy, a new team member. They have been on a motorbike together visiting a village in Khmer Rouge controlled territory on the edge of Highway Five. It is safe enough in the daytime but not safe at night. The bike has broken down.

Krom Akphiwat Phum has this week acquired a Toyota from a grant through OSB; it has a blue flag, a radio and the Krom logo painted on the side. Ka volunteers to drive this ute to rescue our friends who are, it seems, sheltering in a ditch at the side of the road. 'If I am kidnapped you can get me back with a few bags of rice. If a barang was kidnapped,' Ka shakes his head at me, 'it would cost us a thousand dollars. You stand by the radio.'

Ka keeps transmitting radio signals. There is no signal from Nee or Soeuy; I suspect that their radios are switched off. I continue to call. 'Oscar Bravo One ... Oscar Bravo Six.' No response.

Late in the night there is still no news; I am keeping contact with Ka but there has been nothing from the other two since their first distress call; it is reasonable that they should be cautious about revealing their location. Ka is driving backwards and forwards along the stretch of road where they last signalled, then further along into Khmer Rouge held territory. I bring the radio to my house in Wat Kundung.

Monee and I stand together in the starlight under the jackfruit tree listening for signals. There is a good, clear message from Ka but still nothing from Soeuy or Nee.

'Oscar Bravo One, Oscar Bravo One, look for Toyota with logo passing you on the highway. Over.' Time and again we hear no response.

Monee says, 'He is a strong man. He will be alright.'

'You always tell me that what you like about him is that he is gentle.'

'Strong and gentle,' she says.

'Oscar Bravo Base. Oscar Bravo Base this is Oscar Bravo Two. Found them. Over and Out.'

22

THE YEAR THAT DREW US BACKWARDS

The Khmer Rouge troops are once again advancing on Battambang. Hun Sen accuses FUNCINPEC of colluding with them. In February, 1997 is already shaping into a troubled year.

I visit Lum Aung in her office in the National Assembly near the Royal Palace. There is little I can do to support her. Seeing her whenever I come to Phnom Penh is no more than a gesture of friendship. Though navigating deep waters, she is still idealistic.

'Remember Cabramatta?' I say as I greet her in her office. I am remembering how we recently met when we were both in Australia. It may not have been as remarkable for her as it was for me. Lum Aung had asked me to go with her on the train from Milsons Point, where she was staying on the affluent North Shore, representing Cambodia at a conference. Sihanouk supporters had asked her to come to meet them at a club in Cabramatta, a suburb north-west of Sydney, home to a large Asian community.

On a Saturday night, after her work at the conference was finished, we reached Cabramatta Station close to midnight then we threaded our way to the club. The directions we were following led to a dark alleyway. I bustled my carefully groomed companion to the only well-lit doorway, hoping that we had reached the chosen place. We stepped through into the light and immediately, before she could open her mouth, Lum Aung was greeted with a standing ovation. She moved to a dais and began to speak. The club was crowded with many of the listeners standing. They absorbed every word she said.

Here in her office in Phnom Penh Lum Aung brushes talk of Cabramatta aside. She is worried about the growing tension between the FUNCINPEC and the CPP. From the time that the election result was patched together there has been strain between the two prime ministers: Prince Ranariddh and Mr Hun Sen. There is real danger that armed conflict will spread across the country once again.

$$\Omega$$

Every year the Krom Akphiwat Phum team takes a week away from Battambang to reflect on what has happened and to plan for what is next. We are finishing breakfast in a small café at the back of the Royal Palace in Phnom Penh.

It is Easter Sunday morning: clear, early, sunny. We are on the way to Sihanoukville. The noodle soup, rich with chicken and topped with fried garlic and chilli, is, we all agree, particularly delicious. These friends have known starvation and I enjoy watching them relishing good food. Our meals are inevitably silent. I respect this concentration on what they are eating. 'We have a meal to eat, not to talk.'

This must be the fifth year we have taken time away for reflection and planning. I am thoughtful; Easter Sunday is, for me, the culmination of the Holy Week theme of Jesus' death and resurrection, of light overcoming darkness. The twelve Cambodians are looking forward to arriving at the beach.

Ean calls for the bill. He frowns in concentration as he looks from the invoice on the table to the calculator in his hand. If this was happening in Australia I would be embarrassed. Here I grin and tease fondly. If Ean can ever find an inconsistency in the bill he is delighted. It won't matter whether he finds we are undercharged or overcharged: he will point it out to the waiter in a manner so friendly that nobody needs to lose face.

Our next meal will be seafood by the sea.

There comes the sound of an explosion nearby. In an instant the morning shatters. I hold my breath. Three more explosions come, each following closely on the one before. Then movement begins again.

The waiter says that he thinks some garment workers are demonstrating in front of the palace or over near the National Assembly. Since trade unions began in the factories earlier in the year, there have been many demonstrations. The police are often heavy-handed in their reaction. I worry about such young women with so much to lose; everywhere that the poor stand for their rights there are brave or naive people with everything to lose.

Our route to the coast does not take us in the direction of the demonstration. We cram into the ute and set out. The very simple guest house where we stay has no TV. It is Monday before we are confronted with the images on CNN.

We see, against the backdrop of the Royal Palace, body parts littered across the road, the dying lying with the dead. There is an image of a very young girl. Her long hair is soaked with blood. Her face is frozen in shock and bewilderment. Her legs are missing. She is trying to stand up. Later she dies. We piece together the information we can find.

WRITING FOR RAKSMEY

This was planned as a peaceful political demonstration led by the opposition leader Sam Rainsy. He has been supporting exploited young garment workers. The newspapers report that the small group of demonstrators carried placards: 'Down with the Communist Judiciary' and 'Stop the Theft of State Assets'. They had gained official permission for their demonstration. Troops in full riot gear came from a nearby street and encircled them. Persons who are never named threw grenades into the demonstration. It is reported that at least sixteen are dead and one hundred and fifty injured.

After the first grenade was thrown, Sam Rainsy's guard threw himself on top of his leader. He died; Rainsy was protected from the next barrage of grenades. Onlookers claimed that the men in uniform, identified as members of Hun Sen's bodyguard, impeded those who tried to pursue the attackers, that some then blocked bystanders from rushing to the aid of the injured.

By the time we hear of this there is already international reaction. We talk of the contrast between this and the total lack of coverage of the massacre in the Mong district in Battambang Province. The heartbreak of the attack on the train to Battambang rated not a mention even in the local press; there were no eyewitnesses. During this horror bystanders recorded images that could be flashed across the world.

Ω

A US citizen is among the injured. He is medevaced out of the country. Family and friends of the Cambodians who died honour them where they fell. This is a new gesture. People bring flowers

THE YEAR THAT DREW US BACKWARDS

and set them on the blood-darkened soil. The authorities remove the flowers. People bring more. Again they are removed.

In the decades of dying there has not been the chance for any of the factions to publicly honour their dead. I recall Nee's childhood memory. Someone who came to the family to whisper the story of his father's death first whispered, 'You must not cry. The family will be punished if you cry.' I wonder whether the tears and flowers for the March '97 dead may in some way serve to honour them all.

We sit, the Krom team and I, on a blue plastic tarpaulin in a quiet place close to the sea. We remember village people who have risked their lives for the sake of justice. We remember the Battambang train.

We remember the dead.

$$\Omega$$

In mid-year the pressure peaks. The political tensions between the two parties of the reluctant coalition have become irreconcilable. There are even growing strains between CPP members and their leader Hun Sen. Some CPP politicians are sandbagging their Phnom Penh homes.

I am worried for Lum Aung. She is making plans for her mother's safety but she intends to go nowhere. 'Look,' she says. 'I have no husband or children depending on me. I can stand firm for what is right. No need for me to run.' I nod, though I worry. 'Same as you,' she says.

On July 4th Prime Minister Ranariddh of FUNCINPEC flees to France. Lum Aung stays in Phnom Penh.

There are two days of fierce fighting in the capital. The CNN channel shows frightened civilians scampering and hiding from the crossfire. Troop carriers patrol the streets, major thoroughfares are blocked. Soldiers are using shoulder-held rocket launchers. Airlines halt flights to and from Cambodia. Thirty thousand Cambodians flee to Thailand. They include many FUNCINPEC members of parliament and their families. By the evening of July 6th FUNCINPEC soldiers, still officially part of the army of the nation, are routed with a huge loss of lives and many arrests.

In August the United Nations Centre for Human Rights in Cambodia publishes a report: 'Memorandum to the Royal Government of Cambodia: evidence of summary executions, torture and missing persons since 2–7 July 1997'. They document '41 and possibly up to 60 politically motivated extrajudicial executions'. Stories of torture are detailed.

Nobody knows where Lum Aung is; she has not left the country. She is moving from house to house: she knows that other members of the government have been found and executed.

The site of the grenade is once more the place to lay flowers for the dead, even though authorities routinely clear flowers away.

$$\Omega$$

Within three years a stone stupa will be erected to mark this place. Two days after the stupa is completed it is found in a sewerage outlet at the edge of the lake. Supporters, those who remember the dead, retrieve it and set it back in place. The following month it is destroyed where it stands: 'Pounded to rubble.'

It is rebuilt within two weeks. This time it is taken in the night and thrown into the Mekong from the new Japanese Friendship Bridge. It is re-erected the very next morning and ground to dust in the afternoon. Later that same afternoon supporters erect a new stupa placing ashes of the dead and a Buddha statue inside. A bulldozer is used to crush this one. People are injured in the surrounding chaos.

The US Ambassador requests the King Father, Norodom Sihanouk, to intervene. Finally the municipality grants permission for a new stupa. It is completed in August 2000.

Ω

An inscription reads:

> To the heroic demonstrators who lost their lives on March 30th 1997
> for the cause of justice and democracy.
> The tragedy occurred 60 meters from this monument
> on the sidewalk of the park across from the National Assembly.
>
> Chet Duong Dara, medical doctor/journalist, 29
> Hann Muny, bodyguard, 32
> Yung Srey, female garment worker, 21
> Yos Siem, female garment worker, 36
> Sam Sarin, bicycle repairer, 50
> Ros Sir, high school boy, 17
> Yung Sok Nov, female garment worker, 20
> Chea Nang, high school teacher (passer-by) 28
> Nam Thy, motordop driver, 37
> Chanty Pheakdey, high school girl, 13
> Unknown others.

The Cambodia Daily in reporting this adds a postscript: 'We remember your courage and will not forget you for "remembrance is the only paradise out of which we cannot be driven away" (Jean Paul Richter).'

Ω

Toul Sleng, a few kilometres across the city from this monument, is the prison where some sixteen thousand inmates were tortured. Most died under torture; some survived to be executed later. It is all recorded meticulously. At least six thousand images of children, women and men are preserved; many are photographed before and after torture. This evokes horror; there has been no resolution. It is the scene of a crime, not a memorial.

Village after village throughout the country has a killing field where the bones of the brave and the bones of the innocent lie covered with a thin layer of earth. In a cave of the mountain Phnom Sampeu in Battambang Province there is an open pit of bones, some with rotting clothing still clinging.

Most Cambodians of the generation who suffered shrink from these places.

When US military officials asked permission of the Cambodian Government to search for bones of a few American soldiers missing in action, Hun Sen aptly replied that they were welcome but would find that his country had too many bones.

Ω

THE YEAR THAT DREW US BACKWARDS

The Krom team talk to me seriously as the country prepares for the second election to be held in July 1998. 'Help our people to be brave enough to vote,' they say. 'Be an official election watcher. Do this for our country,' they say.

I cannot comprehend the courage that is needed to persevere with democratic elections.

Ω

A young American doctor and I arrive at one of our allotted polling booths early.

It is 6 am; I am an 'accredited observer' with my identification pinned to my shirt and my checklist in my hands. My task is to observe and to ask questions if I need to, but not to challenge or to touch anything.

Election day in the first booth has a carnival atmosphere even at this early hour. There is music. Crowds of men and women waiting to vote watch through the lattice window as the small timber classroom is prepared for voting. The chairman of the five-person Polling Station Committee upends a tin ballot box stamped 'Donation from Japan'. The observers in the booth and the watchers through the window are shown that it is empty. Then it is locked, sealed and made ready.

The booth opens to the waiting queue at 7 am. Most of the men who sit behind the tables to administer the ballot are schoolteachers. They maintain order in a way that seems to me obsessive: there is one correct way to fold the ballot paper, one correct way to place it in the box, one correct way to dip one's finger into the indelible ink to prevent re-voting. None of the voters seem daunted.

Women with babes in arms and children clinging to their sarongs approach the cardboard shelter of the polling booth with reverence. A young man with an infected leg heavily bandaged hops unaided across the room on his muscular healthy leg. A blind man is guided by the chairman.

The ballot paper has thirty-nine party logos, each with a party name below it. Many of the voters are illiterate; the task is to make a mark, any mark, close to the logo of the party of choice.

My colleague and I ask questions and record answers without knowing whether what we are told is naive or sinister.

'I am recording the voters in pencil instead of pen because pencil is easier to rub out.'

'I am guiding the voters' hands while they put their ballot in the box because many do not understand that the fold of the paper must face towards them.'

'I am tearing off plenty of ballot papers from my stub and stamping and folding them in advance because many more people may still come to vote.'

We spend time in each of eleven polling stations in a remote location then watch the sealed boxes with their official papers brought to a central location after the polls close. When we hurry to Battambang to radio our observations to Phnom Penh we are told that the result has already been declared to the world. This was a free and fair election.

My American friend returns to his country; he gives me his tape of the music of *Les Miserables*.

23

TWO FAMILIES

Thalika joins the Krom Akphiwat Phum team. He moves to live closer to Battambang town and invites me to a meal with his family.

Small dwellings are packed narrowly together in this poorer neighbourhood. Thalika's quadriplegic brother, Thy, is lying on a bamboo bench unable to sit upright or to talk. His eyes are alert. He remembers me and makes grumphing sounds of welcome from deep in his throat.

I remember the day in Site 2 when Thalika first had news that his soldier brother had been brought in from the jungle critically ill. We thought he had been injured, but found that he had been paralysed by a rare virus. There is no cure.

Thalika's wife Ha is gently attentive to Thy, feeding him with a spoon, bathing him, washing his clothes. She tells me that Lud has designed a chair for him so that he can be propped upright; a carpenter in town is making it. This might resolve problems with pressure sores.

There are three little boys now. They play happily on the mat, catching their father's attention, watching his every move. Ha is preparing food over a charcoal fire near the doorway; this small house has no upstairs. The family has invited Thalika's friend from the next house to eat with us. He speaks English, as does Thalika.

Ha speaks only Khmer. The two men chat with me as we wait for the rice to be ready. I try to switch to Khmer and to draw Ha into the conversation but she is shy and Thalika's friend is fascinated by my Australian English. His teachers did not have this accent.

I watch Ha's dignity, her calm handling of all of the tasks: Thalika's brother, the food, the children, the hospitality. I judge that she may be a little older than Thalika and very likely a village woman. She is dressed in a faded sarong and an unadorned tee-shirt, her straight hair pulled back from her face. Thalika depends on her for the care his brother will always need.

We sit on the floor-mat and share the meal. Ha and the little boys eat with us though Ha is constantly looking to ensure that her husband, the children and the guests have all that they need. There is rice which we flavour with food from one of the three serving dishes: fried vegetables, small rice-field fish grilled over charcoal, chicken broth. It is eleven thirty in the morning; this is the first and main meal of the day.

Before the meal is over the neighbour's small daughter is brought into our circle to say 'Hello' to me in English. Ha's sober face breaks into a smile. I look around the gathering and understand that normally Ha is the lone woman in this male household of Thalika, Thy and the three young sons. The little girl is special to her.

Ω

The Krom team has an evening celebration in the salla. They are just finishing assembling a book of stories from the villages. It has large black-and-white photographs and simple Khmer script. It is written to help the people of the villages to be proud of their achievements.

TWO FAMILIES

Everybody on the team has helped to gather the stories, and everybody is excited.

The tiled floor is cleared of mats. There is a table of drinks in the corner: Fanta, Sprite and Angkor Beer. Popular Cambodian music is turned to the loudest volume and we are dancing. I look around for Thalika. He is still in the computer booth putting finishing touches to the book before sending it to the printer. 'C'mon,' I say.

The dancing is half classical Khmer, half Western. Each dancer moves alone to the music. Thalika joins the crowded floor and finds his rhythm. His feet shift position slightly, keeping time with the music while not leaving the tiled floor. His hands bend backwards in classical pose moving with the music to shape images in the air. We watch amazed then Touern, irrepressible, makes exuberant dance movements around him. When the music finishes we clap and Thalika goes back to the computer.

This is some of the best classical dancing I have seen. Did he learn it from his Uncle Soeun? Surely not in Site 2. Who were his parents? What was their story?

$$\Omega$$

A message comes for Thalika while the team is having the annual retreat at Kompong Som. The little daughter of his neighbor has died. It is a sad loss; this little girl is like family to him. Nee sits with him and listens. Though Thalika feels great sadness he decides to stay until the end of the retreat. When he is back home in Battambang he will give money for the thirty-day ceremony for the child.

Almost a month after the child has died Ha is arrested for her murder and is imprisoned in the Battambang goal. Nobody has an explanation that we know of. Now there is anguish in Thalika's household as well as in the house next door. The children are crying for their mother. Thalika's brother is distraught, Thy cannot talk about what he is suffering or tell about anything he may have seen. Thalika must now feed and clothe and care for Thy; his children also need his care. His close friend in the next door house blames Thalika and does not invite him to the thirty-day ceremonies. Thalika listens to the mourning music and grieves alone.

Battambang gaol is a dark and crowded place. When Thalika visits his wife he brings her food but cannot ease her misery and bewilderment. Some prisoners here have waited ten years without trial. Possibly because Thalika is connected to the expat community Ha has her trial after only six months. She is judged to be innocent of any crime but fears showing her face in Battambang, and disappears into Phnom Penh.

Thy is still distressed and cannot settle. Thalika is doing all he can for his brother and his children but within a year Thy dies. Eventually the sons go to live close to their mother in Phnom Penh. Thalika is alone.

He spends more and more time in his villages talking into the night with the leaders he is mentoring.

$$\Omega$$

In the few years following the tragedy of the arrest of his wife and the death of his brother, Thalika adds decades to his age. Even when I meet him amidst the comradery at Krom his face is always sad. I try to see him alone whenever I am in Battambang.

TWO FAMILIES

It is Khmer New Year, the great annual celebration when families come together. Thalika and I arrange to meet for a meal. He wants to take me to a restaurant but those that are not closed for the holiday are packed with revellers. We cannot find traditional New Year delicacies for our meal but sit together with a simple meal and a glass of beer. It is easier to talk of the future than of the past.

Thalika's sons are musical. They would like to make music their career. Thalika laughs at last, insisting that before they depend on dubious opportunities to form a band to make a living they should be educated and ready for a 'real job'.

He is guiding his children's future while living alone. He sees them when he can and they are close to their mother. His friend, the bereaved father, has never reconciled with him.

$$\Omega$$

One late afternoon Nee and I are sitting on the bench beneath my house, talking. He has spent most of the week in the distant village of Tanak. The people there suffered greatly during Khmer Rouge times and, though their village is now notionally controlled by the government during the day, they are attacked at night by Khmer Rouge troops who come down from the hills demanding food and raping women. 'I understand life there,' he says. 'I know what it is like.'

We talk about the INGOs in Battambang. Nee now has friends among the expats and from time to time is invited to meet their representatives who travel to Cambodia from overseas headquarters. He tells me that he often meets foreigners of good heart, who are committed to 'bringing development' to Cambodia. He wishes that they could enter into the day and night lives and struggles of ordinary village people, to notice what is happening. There are things that they need to know. He is thinking that if he could write down his own story it might be a way to help them to enter into the hearts of his people. He thinks that we might perhaps work on this together in the evenings or during weekends when there is a chance. Could I help him?

I take time to decide, then I agree.

Ω

Nee is remembering all the details of his life. I am glad to listen and to check that I am hearing his story correctly. Whether or not the words we write will ever be published it seems a good thing for Nee to be able to talk about these things.

We set up a routine of times to meet. He starts with a story his mother told him. Late in her first pregnancy her husband was called into the army. To be a teacher was to be in government service and all in government service could be called by King Sihanouk to military service. Though her husband's battalion was stationed not far from their home he was not permitted to come back, not even for the birth of his first child. The older women who supported her during labour said that this little baby named Nee was beautiful; if she wanted him to live she should keep a sharp knife by his pillow to frighten away the spirit of any mother of an earlier incarnation. He could be snatched back. The monks also warned her of her responsibility to watch the baby until his father came home. She followed their suggestion exactly. She wrapped him in a tattered old piece of saffron-coloured monks' cloth so unattractive that nobody would want to snatch him. She placed a knife beside his pillow.

TWO FAMILIES

Nee tells of his joy as a small boy in a rice field riding on the back of a buffalo. He tells of the Ho Chi Minh trail that ran through his village and into South Vietnam. The tall bamboos sheltered the convoys of armaments that could move carefully along at night without danger of being seen from the air. Any small boy, even though forbidden to be out after dark, could find a way to watch all of this.

Then came the terror of the village becoming frontline, of shells falling as young and old crouched together terrified, of joining with the hordes of Svey Reing families who left everything behind and fled to Phnom Penh for safety.

It seemed that nothing could be harder than struggling for survival on the edge of this city choked with families fleeing the fighting. Then something worse happened. The Khmer Rouge entered the city and sent the family walking back along the road. There was no longer safety for anyone anywhere. His father was killed. The way his father was killed is the hardest thing to talk about.

The vision he now has of bringing healing has grown from all these things that happened before. If life is ever to be lived freely Cambodians will need to gather what is left and build from that. There has to be a Khmer way.

I listen as he speaks, type on the laptop linked to the truck battery, show him what is written, then revise it. We revise until the typed words are precisely what Nee wants to say and can be put between covers and produced in Phnom Penh as a small book.

We choose a name for it: 'Towards Restoring Life'. It spreads in ever-widening circles. There are words that ring true in other places where communities are trying to recover after violence. It is translated into one language after another: Thai, Bahasa Indonesia, French, Spanish, the Karen language and Japanese. We are shown the French, Japanese and Spanish versions before they are published and trust that they are accurate. The copies made in countries where people are struggling as Cambodia is struggling give us the greatest satisfaction. These translations happen spontaneously without any discussion with us. We are glad of whatever way this book might be of use.

There are four editions in English, the last published in Melbourne by OSB. We calculate that there are five thousand copies in English.

Some Cambodian teachers use a Khmer version with their students; it is used for a class in Siem Reap and taken back to Choeuteal village where the story began.

Counterfeit copies of 'Towards Restoring Life' are sold in restaurants and on the streets in Phnom Penh. Nee says, 'No problem. We want them to read it and think about it. We didn't write these things down to earn money.'

$$\Omega$$

I return to my house in Wat Kundung, climb the steps, turn to take a last look at the starlit sky above the jackfruit tree, unlock the door, light my kerosene lamp and bolt the door behind me.

Nee is becoming the thinker and leader that he is capable of being. What is happening is useful for others who have suffered; this is what Nee hopes. What will happen to him?

Can friends like the irrepressible Ka understand? Monee will struggle. His mother and family will probably not think it at all important. Monee's family will think it irrelevant; a distraction from the responsibility to lift the family out of poverty. Too much will be expected of him; more than he can give.

He will be lonely.

TWO FAMILIES

Ω

As it happens, Nee, through a series of unexpected events, is invited to La Trobe University in Australia, to study. He is enrolled at Masters level; once he begins to submit what he is writing he is offered a place at Doctorate level and awarded a scholarship.

His wife and three children join him in Melbourne. He studies day and night, often sleeping on the floor of his university office. He also works for SBS Khmer Language radio in the early mornings in order to support the family and send money back to Cambodia.

The doctorate is complete in three and a half years.

Three days after his graduation ceremony he is back in Cambodia, continuing to work, think, and sleep in the villages, listening to the people. Little has changed, yet everything has.

Yeay cannot reconcile the fact that Nee and the family could have stayed in Australia, that he has limited everyone's chances of a good life by coming back to Cambodia. Why?

It seems to him that he could do no other.

The thesis is about rebuilding communities broken by war. The problem is that the violence is not over. Communities are still shattering.

24

SPANNING THE DISTANCE

My hope is to challenge and encourage Cambodians, to walk beside or behind them, never to take the lead when they are ready to do this for themselves. Friendships will endure, but by the later nineties there is no call for me to stay side by side with Cambodian colleagues whose own leadership is now strong. Responsibilities that I left behind to come to Cambodia claim a share of my life once more. Australian concerns gradually take their place, side by side with Cambodian ones.

Nevertheless, once or twice or even three times a year, when I am invited and am free to do something helpful, I return to Cambodia: publish a book, design a piece of research, coach leaders, guide an annual retreat, participate in planning, oversee an evaluation, strengthen connections with international organisations. There is a sense of continuity and a different style of involvement. If Krom needs support to meet a new challenge and to learn from it I can usually be there. Requests also come from other local and international NGOs.

I am in Battambang in 1999 when Nick Dunlop, while out in a village with a mine-clearing group, realises that he is looking into the face of the man who was in charge of the notorious Toul Sleng prison. Nick is a 32-year-old journalist-photographer who knows recent Cambodian history, carries many images in his mind and, in his pocket, the image of Duch, who has not been seen since the

Vietnamese drove the Khmer Rouge from Phnom Penh. Many presume that Duch is dead.

Kaing Guek Eav, also known as Duch, is wearing an American Refugee Committee tee-shirt when Nick realises that he is shaking the hand of the Toul Sleng torturer. Duch has become a Christian and worked with international NGOs under an assumed name; he would never have expected that the young foreigner whose hand is in his, would know his face.

When Duch is afterwards confronted by Nick and Nate Tayer, a journalist from *The Far Eastern Economic Review*, he confesses. Duch accepts responsibility for the torture and execution of thousands of inmates in Toul Sleng, possibly seventeen thousand, expresses 'heartfelt sorrow' for his crimes, and vows to co-operate fully with the Tribunal.

People say that when Duch was led as a prisoner back to the scenes of his crimes he said, 'I ask you for forgiveness. I know that you cannot forgive me, but ask you to leave me the hope that you might.'

The progress of the Khmer Rouge Tribunal is slow. The concept of an Extraordinary Chambers in the Courts of Cambodia is agreed. Each accused is to have a Cambodian and an international defence lawyer. The co-prosecutors for each case are also balanced: one Cambodian and one international. The responsibility of judges is likewise shared.

Those to be charged will be senior leaders and members of the Khmer Rouge, regarded as most responsible for the crimes committed between 1975 and 1979. Among the people in the villages there remains the memory and sometimes the presence of village people known to be torturers. They will never be confronted with their crimes.

Theary, who travels out to villages for work in women's health, is drawn into this dilemma. A Cambodian woman who comes to her asking for help was a little girl at the time of the terror. She believes that a man who tortured her family members to death is still in the village she fled many years ago. She watched this official commit his atrocities. Though she is afraid to return to the place where her loved ones were killed she wants this man, whose name she recalls, to be confronted with his crime. 'I'm frightened to go myself,' she says to Theary. 'You go to that village for your work. Will you confront him for me?'

A Dutch camera team films the encounter. They win a high award for the documentary that they produce but my attention is on Theary's experience, not their artistry. Theary dares to sit with the accused man and challenge him directly. He is defensive and belligerent at first but she manages to gain his trust. Slowly she realises that this man, Mr Karoby, was and still is illiterate, that he was threatened from further up the line of the tight Khmer Rouge chain of command, that he knows he is hated. The camera keeps returning to his troubled face as he works to change his karma by assisting with funeral rites in the village, taking a leading role in the ceremonies. Guilt and sorrow are heavy.

The camera follows Theary as she reflects time and again with the woman who is seeking for resolution of past horrors, and with Mr Koraby, who carries the burden of guilt.

Theary is looking for understanding. Part of the truth, she says, is that none of us could know what we would do if forced to obey orders by a regime as punitive as the Khmer Rouge. In her mind she returns to the details of her own story. She was an adolescent in Khmer Rouge captivity towards the end of the Pol Pot time. Her captors gave her the responsibility of caring for the younger children. She is grateful that the regime was crushed by the Vietnamese army before she was put to the test ... How would she have endured pressure to obey cruel orders?

After the film is completed and released Theary continues to see Mr Karoby, as she respectfully calls him. She treats him for his high blood pressure until the end of his life.

The gruesome details of torture and death are difficult to hear and see, but it is Theary's own reflections that challenge me most.

$$\Omega$$

Anne Goldfield and Sok Thim have founded an NGO to address the need for treatment of TB sufferers. They have experience and a strong body of knowledge from continuing research. Thim is Executive Director of the NGO that he and Anne founded. They call it the Cambodian Health Committee, CHC. In responding to TB, a disease of poverty, they are rightly alarmed by growing numbers of patients suffering from AIDS. The two are connected, as those with lowered immune systems are vulnerable to TB.

Sok Thim and Anne take me to a remote village close to the Vietnamese border. We stand in burning sunlight while Thim bends over a 60-year-old man whose skin is tight across his skeletal bones. Thim takes his stethoscope, listens intently, then through a gauze mask speaks to the patient.

Gathered close but not too close are family, neighbours, and a 'masked up' community assistant who supervises the patient's daily medication. It is DOTS, daily observed therapy. This work is serious; very serious. The diagnosis is multiple-drug-resistant TB; it is highly contagious and difficult to treat. Thim leans down to the patient, relating to him as the most important person in the world. He congratulates him on his faithfulness to the medication and explains the improvement in his condition. The patient beams a toothless smile.

Thim shares a joke; family and neighbours within hearing laugh too. As he listens again with his stethoscope sweat runs from his forehead into his eyes … He was on the road for four hours before reaching this particular 'bedside'.

I look around me, a fat sow and six or seven piglets lie together in the yard beside us. The patient's bed is a bamboo bench and mosquito net outside a rough timber house, hens scratch close to the bed.

Sok Thim is calm, reassuring and professional. Well he might be; he qualified in Boston and has managed many cures in open-air 'clinics' such as this.

$$\Omega$$

Dr Anne is leading her research team at Harvard while still involved in Cambodia and other places where the need for medical services is extreme. As CHC grows into an organisation reaching many thousands of patients and producing research outcomes with global significance, Anne and Thim invite me to spend some days with them as they adjust to the extra responsibilities and demands to restructure that come from this growth.

CHC specialised in TB treatment from the start. Gradually that led to involvement with the dual diagnosis of TB and HIV/AIDS and the treatment of multiple-drug resistant TB. CHC has developed TB wards in city hospitals and treatment is also taken to patients in remote communities.

SPANNING THE DISTANCE

I sit with Anne and Thim as they make decisions. 'What do you most want to do? How can you manage this?'

They are both specialist physicians and Anne an internationally respected researcher. There is no ambiguity for either of them. They go to the places of greatest suffering and treat illness that would not otherwise be treated. Nobody should be left to suffer and die when a cure is possible.

On the other hand, leading a large organisation involves a constant burden of managing staff and finding funds. Thim accepts it with reluctance; his greatest satisfaction is to take a motorbike to a patient in some remote village and call upon all of his experience and knowledge to achieve a cure.

Anne has been to many countries where suffering is intense and knows that the experience of CHC can be used in impoverished countries beyond Cambodia. She will do whatever it takes.

There is an invitation to set up a program in Ethiopia. While I ask 'How can you manage this?' they are already planning. They can and they will succeed. 'Failure is not an option.' People are suffering from lethal but curable infectious disease. CHC in Ethiopia will be called the Global Health Committee.

$$\Omega$$

In a villa on a backstreet in Phnom Penh small children are climbing on play equipment, shouting, giggling, taking risks as children do. Anne and Thim have brought me to this part of the CHC program.

There is clean sand to cover the dusty ground and to cushion a fall. Older boys and girls sit in the shade of trees or along the edge of the veranda. Some are still arriving for the day. They come on motorbikes in the way that families with enough money would want their children to travel. The motor-dup drivers are paid weekly by CHC. Everything here gives the impression of normality. There is food being cooked in the kitchen.

A team of professional Cambodian medics, teachers, counsellors and social workers is based in this friendly place, the Maddox Chivers Children's Centre of the Cambodian Health Committee. They provide all that is possible for three hundred AIDS-infected and affected children and their families. My task here is to bring this group of professionals into conversation, each appreciating the contribution of the others and setting case plans with a family focus.

Before the work of the day begins I squat down at the level of the children and begin to talk to them. They gather around. One little boy snuggles in to me and fastens his arms around my waist. He will not let go.

During my time of working at the Maddox Centre he follows me around like a shadow.

$$\Omega$$

New members have joined the Krom Akphiwat Phum team; some of the original team are still there. The leadership is now consistently six women and six men. The central co-ordinating group of three is still elected by all twelve when the time comes for leadership to rotate. The work has extended to many villages in districts across the province. The direction is still shaped by listening to the people of the village and building on their strengths, responding to their hopes. The variety of projects people in the villages choose to undertake still surprises me: agriculture of all kinds, adult literacy, schools for children, music groups, drama groups, roads, bridges, the raising of small and large animals, support groups for the poor in the village and for those suffering domestic violence, health care, consciousness raising about justice, human rights, rule of law, protests about false imprisonment and land grabbing. The Krom team tells me, 'All the people in the villages want survival and a better life for their families, while we support the projects they choose we want to strengthen trust, co-operation and good leadership. This is the way lasting change will happen.'

I travel out on the motorbikes to villages we knew in the beginning, tasting the joy of seeing the way that leadership has developed and that life has become better. I stay nights in villages of long-time friends and know that the struggles with poverty and oppression are still a challenge.

I am invited to return to Spean. The people have a co-operative agriculture program that they would like me to see. We sit in an open pavilion under the shade of a tin roof listening to an animated discussion of new ways of planting a seedbed, setting straight lines, measuring distances. The wooden floor is an uncomfortable place to sit for a long discussion though from here I can see that some fine timber houses have replaced 'straw houses' of a decade or so ago. Monks are chanting under a wooden house nearby. A young woman at the top of the stairs has food to bring down to them. She pauses to slip a sarong over her bright orange shorts then demurely descends the ladder.

I feel a finger tapping my shoulder, and turn; it is a young man with a handful of flowers from the fields. He mouths some words for welcome in Khmer and holds the flowers towards me. On cue the former village leader arrives. He has a new role now as master of ceremonies at weddings, and he seems to think that this, or his earlier role as village leader, entitles him to interrupt the agricultural meeting. He is wearing a patterned silk jacket which must surely be what he wears for weddings. He thanks me for coming back to Spean then launches proudly into the story of the day he rescued me when I fell from the wet log. We both have some grey hairs now.

Ω

While the Black Saturday bushfires are still raging in the Victorian countryside, I am walking along Pin Oak Crescent in Flemington. There is a smoke haze over Melbourne. I am tense as I listen to 24-hour radio warnings of new flare-ups of fires. I have friends and family living in various trouble-spots in the bush and wish I could be sure that they have left for safety rather than opting to stay to fight the fire.

My mobile phone rings. 'Yeay this is Raksmey.' This is the first time he has ever phoned me. I stand still in the smoky dusk listening to the worry in Raksmey's voice.

'Raksmey where are you?'

'Phnom Penh. I think my father is dying.'

'What is it?'

'He is badly injured. He is unconscious.'

'Where is he?'

'In the hospital. He made me drive him around until we could find a doctor he could trust. I think he will die.'

'Who is with him? Are you alone with him in the hospital?'

'Yes'

SPANNING THE DISTANCE

I try to hear the facts as well as the anxiety. It seems that Nee has had emergency surgery; unconscious may mean not yet out of anaesthetic.

'Smey my phone is charged and turned on. Text me when you need to talk and I will phone you back. Your father chose the doctor he could trust?'

'Yes. He was conscious then.'

'We should trust that doctor too.'

We stay in contact, Smey and I, this week and the next, and the next. Nee is recovering from surgery, his leg is smashed behind the knee-cap, the doctor he so carefully chose has inserted a metal rod. Nee's colleagues gathered around his hospital bed are convinced that the accident has been made to happen because of his work for oppressed peoples, and that it was actually an attack. Stories swirl.

Nee and the family say that it was just an accident.

$$\Omega$$

Smey has grown into a thoughtful young man. In 2012 he drives me to Battambang and asks me about Site 2. If knowing the story will help Smey I will of course look back at what I wrote at the time of the camp and write for him.

Nee has a house in Phnom Penh, Proan Pra. He urges me to stay with him and his sons whenever I am in the city. Reaksa and Raksmey welcome this; their father is often out in villages for days or even weeks.

Yeay is alone now in the house we all once shared in Battambang. She has encouraged and helped Monee and Srey Leak to find security in the USA. Srey Leak met Siem in Battambang when he was holidaying in Cambodia. He has persuaded Srey Leak to stay in Minnesota. Monee lives with them.

While in the USA for a meeting I travel to Minnesota. Through mutual friends Siem hears that I am there and arranges to meet me in St Paul and drive me to Rochester, several hours away across the state. He wants to surprise Srey Leak by having me there in the car when she finishes her evening shift at work. On the way Siem and I talk. He was born in the UNHCR refugee camp on Cambodia's border and his rice-farmer parents arrived in the USA with their young children almost without trying to be there. Siem has a master's degree in engineering.

Srey Leak is as delighted as Siem hoped she would be. So is Monee. I stay with them all there in Rochester: Srey Leak, Monee and Siem. In Walmart Srey Leak and I phone Nee. Monee remembers that I loved the way she prepared fried rice and she cooks it exactly as before.

Part III

Bringing Back the Stories

25

THE KING FATHER IS DEAD

Friends email from the USA to alert me. February 4th 2013 will surely be a day that traffic in Cambodia's capital will be impossible. His Royal Highness, Norodom Sihanouk, God-King to the villagers, King-Father to educated Cambodian city people, is to be cremated. It is the third and final day of the cremation ceremony. There have been 100 days between the death and the cremation.

I have come to bring back the stories, not to witness the cremation of the King-Father. In my bag are print-outs of what I have written down: a section for this family, a section for that. I negotiated for award flights with Qantas: arrival February 4th 2013, departure March 15th 2013. The dates are significant beyond my expectation.

The wait in transit at Changi Airport in Singapore is long. The conversation in the gate lounge for departure to Phnom Penh is mostly in Khmer. Other passengers waiting for this early morning flight are Cambodians flying home from the vast diaspora of Cambodians from around the world. Whatever I may think of Norodom Sihanouk, His Royal Highness is certainly not insignificant.

As we wait we watch a large screen with images of the Cambodian Royal Palace, of the Killing Fields, and of the man who has died. King Sihanouk is speaking to the camera, always speaking. This ebullient little man certainly had great gifts, as well as flaws. On vintage film clips we watch him take astonishing gambles to protect a future for his country. He played politics relentlessly. Though for some years he chose a political career over kingship he never ceased to mix both roles.

His Highness was merciless in imprisoning, torturing and ridiculing enemies. Always so. He lost three of his many children and fourteen of his grandchildren to the Pol Pot reign of terror even as he lived with the Khmer Rouge leaders in the palace in an emptied Phnom Penh: first as a figurehead leader, then as a man under house arrest. He made alliances with the Khmer Rouge more than once.

We passengers are unusually subdued: thoughtful as we board the plane for the last stage of our journey from Singapore to Phnom Penh.

The jostling queue for 'visa on arrival' is familiar; I am ready. Beyond the cool dimness of the Pochentong Airport Customs Hall, out at the edge of the glare of morning sunlight, a larger than usual crowd waits to greet the arriving passengers. I can see only silhouettes. As I walk through the gate four arms are waving to me.

Nee is there. I thought he was in Ratanakiri. Beside him is Reaksa, free from university for the day of cremation. I step into familiar welcome.

Reaksa still calls me Yeay. His elder brother Raksmey, who is in Siem Reap today, now calls me Joan.

Nee drives; his son wants to tell me about Sihanouk and I want to listen to what he understands. There will be time for Nee and I to talk later.

Reaksa and his friends from the university are following Facebook and YouTube, watching television and, for the first time in their lives, debating about politics. In the days between Norodom Sihanouk's death and his cremation the Cambodian television channels have been playing documentaries of his life, documentaries previously not permitted. Reaksa has been watching these forty-year-old films over and over. 'There was healthcare for poor people, they could go to good hospitals,' he says. 'When there was a flood or a drought the King was there to help them. Did you know that?'

Astounding, I think. An old man now dead is spreading a political message to a bright young generation. King Sihanouk was a filmmaker in his time; anything that he left behind in archives will show him at his best.

$$\Omega$$

Reaksa buys me the badge of mourning: a circular laminated image of Sihanouk mounted on black and white ribbons. He asks his girl cousin to pin it to my tee-shirt; it is as decorative as a corsage. His own tee-shirt is bright aqua and carries the words 'BE WILD'. His mother sent it to him from the USA. His well-cut curly hair frames a face eager for excitement. We set out on his motorbike.

There is a heavy presence of armed military police close to the Royal Palace, the House of Parliament and the crematorium. Police bark messages into two-way radios. Standing in clusters in their khaki coloured uniforms with tight trousers tucked into shiny black boots, guns at the hip, the red white and blue insignia of the Cambodian flag attached to their sleeves and to their peaked caps, they wait. They walk up and down beside metal barricades freshly painted in red and white.

THE KING FATHER IS DEAD

The barricades, blazing in the sunlight, hold back the villagers who adore the dead one. These rural people travelled in the backs of open trucks. Some sold possessions for the fare. From where they now stand blocked by the police they can see nothing. They came from distant places dressed carefully for the occasion. The women wear long-sleeved white tops, some embroidered or made from lace. The men wear white business shirts, sleeves to their wrists, top collar button open. To put aside rice-field clothes and to dress with dignity they have spent more than they can afford, though they are not treated with dignity. They sweat under the relentless sun.

Many of the older people who now push against the barricades hoping for a glimpse of the place where the coffin lies in state remember the 'Sihanouk time' as the only good time of their lives. Later there was Lon Nol, then Pol Pot, now Prime Minister Hun Sen. 'Same cart, different driver,' they sometimes mutter in private.

Mourning music surrounds and follows everyone in Phnom Penh on this day. It comes from the cremation site; it comes from the continuous television coverage; it is in the air that everyone must breathe.

Norodom Sihanouk's presence is everywhere. We are dwarfed by massive roadside portraits of His Highness: as an eighteen-year-old ascending the throne in 1941, as a young man, triumphant from the achievement of independence from the French in 1953, as a husband of the elegant Monineath who, from among his many wives, continues to be honoured.

At three in the afternoon we hear that official mourners, high-ranking Cambodians and leaders from many countries, are filing through the custom-built crematorium to pay last respects. The villagers still wait by the barricades, occasionally surging forward and being pushed back. Reaksa is on his motorbike looking for a chance to slip between the barricades to a vantage point.

Just after six o'clock in the evening the King, Norodom Sihamoni, and the Queen Mother, Monineath, each light a candle. Their role is to bring their candles into contact with the oil-soaked sandalwood coffin. The curtains of the elaborate crematorium move together to block the view so that the final moments in the atrium cannot be observed by the cameras.

Those who wait outside greet the start of the smoke with silent respect. A 101-gun artillery salute is heard throughout the city. Fireworks explode to honour the life that is over. Even now the ordinary people are restrained; they stand pressed against each other in grief.

Reaksa leaves on his motorbike, weaving and circling to find a way to see more, sending texts to my mobile phone. It is already dark when he finds a way through the barricades; he will bring me there.

The people who have stood waiting all day have found this new opening too. They surge forward in a white-clad crowd. We park the bike and are carried along with them around the Ministry of Arts building, past the stupa commemorating protestors slain in the grenade attack. We stand where we can watch the palace glowing with golden lights. There is a large screen replaying the events of the day.

At a makeshift shrine Reaksa buys me two bunches of deep-pink long-stemmed lotus flowers, painstakingly prepared with their outer petals folded backwards. 'One bunch for each side,' he instructs, 'five incense sticks to put into the urn at a time. What will you pray?'

'I will pray for peace in Cambodia, in our hearts and in the whole world.'

'Same as me,' he says.

THE KING FATHER IS DEAD

Close to us a line of ageing women move through the throng, singing. They seem to be heading towards a truck that will return them to their village. It is difficult to distinguish any words. 'Is it Buddhist chant Reaksa?'

'No, not monk's language. Women cannot sing monk's language. They are singing in Khmer. They are singing thanks and we are proud to be Cambodian.'

26

SOK THIM

We have arranged to meet in Street 278, Sok Thim and I, in mid-February before we each leave Phnom Penh. It is a convenient location for us both. Thim travels to Svey Reing and I to Battambang. There is a quiet café where we will not meet anyone we know, we can talk without interruption about the stories of Thim's life that I have printed at Officeworks, bound together, and given back to him.

Thim has arrived first. He is tapping at his iPad, cool in a fresh short-sleeved shirt with collar unbuttoned. He is bent over the screen, nodding, reaching for the coffee cup without interrupting his reading.

The sunlight flickers through the wall of tall green plants that shields this tiled veranda from the sight of life on the street outside. The cane bucket chairs are padded with cushions: silk-covered, colour-coordinated, all shades of green. I stand in the doorway looking around. A huge terracotta pot sits before me on the tiled floor. It is a pond where tiny fish swim and flowers float. The fragrance of jasmine mingles with the smell of coffee. There is soft music playing: it is jazz.

Twenty years ago I knew this district well. Then the street was a street of simple houses with the benches of vendors clustered at this corner.

Thim hears my greeting and looks up with a smile that has not changed: mischievous. He has taken his two young sons to a school close by. There is a car with the CHC logo parked outside the café. The driver is waiting to take Thim to distant places. He calls the waiter so that I can order, then points to the screen of his iPad to read 'his part' of what I have written. He is serious now.

'I'm not sorry for the life I went through,' he says. 'Somebody who has stepped in the mud can rise up.' He gestures to himself. 'If these things had not happened to me I wouldn't be me.'

Here in this place, where waiters dressed in black trousers and shirts and forest-green starched aprons speak English, where ceiling fans whir, where the emphasis is on catering for foreigners, we talk about suffering and rising from it.

Thim has recently returned from Ethiopia. The Global Health Committee aspect of the work demands his attention, the Ethiopia partnership is expanding. CHC works with the Department of Health and with two hospitals. He sighs as he tells me that setting up the programs and ensuring that the details are in place exhausts him, even though he is proud of the cures already happening there. I know that after the pressure of these things today's chance to work with village patients will be like a well-earned holiday for Thim.

'Do you remember when I asked you about your vision for the Global Health Committee?' I ask. We laugh together. We recall it exactly: 'Go to where suffering is greatest, to treat diseases most difficult to treat.'

As we share a plate of cut mango and pineapple we remember the evening when Thim looked across to Cambodia and talked of the way that the spirit of his people had become very low. For a short time he is silent and still: then he begins to talk about spirit being the centre of everything. 'It is like the central shoot of the banana plant. All the leaves and all the fruit depend on it.'

With this thought between us, Thim starts on a story he has never before told me.

There was shelling close to Site 2 and the KPNLF force was planning a counter-attack. The patients receiving treatment for TB carried written permission to be exempt from military service. This did not deter the military commanders. The patients were rounded up and loaded into army trucks. Thim argued that this was a broken promise, a breach of contract, not acceptable. He began to drag the patients back out of the truck. The commander pulled a gun and held it to his head. 'Fine', Thim said, 'kill me if you want to.'

Thim's smile has vanished now; he leans forward on the table. 'To free yourself you have to control your fear and believe in what you are doing. Otherwise you are stuck in a pool fighting with yourself.'

A waiter comes and offers us the menu again. 'Later,' Thim waves him away. There is silence, then: 'When I was UNBRO Advisor for TB in all the border camps I had to travel to Bangkok to report on this work at a UN meeting. As I walked through the gate of the camp the Thai guards called out "Dog of the barang". During the meeting in Bangkok I wanted very much to say, "I am Cambodian. We know you don't respect us. We have no country, no government. But we still have our dignity."'

There was of course no chance for him to say this.

'Dignity, dignity,' he says. He is looking at me intently. 'The rice distribution in the camp was without dignity. I must take my two small boys to sit in a row under the hot sun.'

He pushes further back into his store of memories. In the mobile youth team in Pol Pot time members of the group disappeared one by one or two at a time to be taken away and killed by the Khmer Rouge. Thim recalls that his belief about dignity and freedom was already strong, even though he was young. 'Don't tie me up. Don't count my head. Kill me when I run but don't tie my hands.'

'This is about spirit,' he says. 'It is about the dignity and freedom of a person.'

He calls for more coffee and I join him in this. At our table in a quiet corner I am jotting in a notebook. Thim encourages me to write down what he is saying, and we part resolving that when we meet again I will give him a print-out of what I have written. Thim wants his story recorded for his two youngest sons. They are fine, thoughtful boys; one day they will need to be told these things.

We step away from this strange oasis. Thim will set out to see his patients, I will prepare for tomorrow's journey to Battambang. Outside our green bunker the road is congested with expensive cars and motorbikes. I smell petrol and the dust of building sites.

$$\Omega$$

Thim waits for me again in the leafy restaurant; he takes the pages I have typed from our earlier meeting, nodding and smiling at what he reads. 'Life is designed,' he says.

His life is busy day after day. The General Department of Prisons in Cambodia has requested the Cambodian Health Committee to take over and expand the TB and Drug Resistant TB program in two large Phnom Penh prisons, with around three-and-a-half-thousand inmates. The prevalence of TB in the prisons is seven times the rate found in the general population. As well, the Global Health Committee partners, the Ethiopian Department of Health, now have responsibility for almost seven hundred Ethiopian patients with drug-resistant TB in that country.

We muse together over the spread of this work. In Cambodia there have been thirty-eight thousand patients in the community care treatment that had its small beginning on the Thai/Cambodia border.

Thim talks of the stress of managing a large staff. The day can start peacefully and before mid-morning be plagued with challenges he could never have imagined. He needs to keep reminding himself that all of this stress comes from doing whatever he can to control unnecessary suffering. 'Love in action,' he says and nods to himself.

He looks back to the stories I have written. He would like to add other things I have not heard before. I laughingly agree; this could go on forever.

Thim tells me that when he was three or four years old his parents, who had quarrelled with each other for years, divorced. Since his mother was a relative of the head monk of a pagoda in Battambang she placed her little boy there to be educated by the monks. 'Threw me there into the Wat,' says Thim. He laughs at this then becomes reflective again. 'It helped to shape my heart.'

The monks supported him in the whole of his education for more than ten years. As well as normal school subjects he learned Sanskrit and Pali. The monks were strict; he needed them to set a high standard. The Buddhist spirit surrounded him and certain beliefs stayed with him. 'Move in the direction you believe. Never be hopeless. There is a door where you don't expect it.'

Right now as he looks back he sees all of this as fortunate. 'In every phase there is wisdom.' He leans back in his chair and chuckles, then talks through laughter. When he was sixteen he went to Phnom Penh, met his parents, and brought them together. Though each had been through 'marriages' since they separated they agreed to marry each other once more. He gained a place at the University of Phnom Penh to begin studying medicine and so it was that when the Khmer Rouge came into Phnom Penh he went in one direction and his parents in another.

We are both laughing. It is the first time I have ever heard the story of the emptying of Phnom told as black humour. In 1979 when Thim found that his parents had gained a place as refugees and had gone to settle in France without him, he decided to start again, with a clean sheet. 'A comrade alone in the world.' He laughs at his young self. Right after he made that decision his parents traced him and wrote to him in the camp. But he was then in trouble with the Cambodian factional authorities of KPNLF. 'Big trouble.' He laughs again.

His parents settled well in France. They tried to bring him there. He is talking and laughing at the same time. As far as the French authorities knew this man and woman had no son. A door closed.

'I'm not sorry for the life I went through,' he says again. A door closes. A door opens.

Thim expects that his life will become simpler one day. He is in his late fifties now and asking himself, 'What do I do with the last part of my life?' But he has an answer. When the time comes this is what he will do: care for the family, be free to choose how to live day by day, end the time of heavy responsibility, still use medical knowledge to care for people, teach at universities, get away from the city to a farm.

'To live small things deeply. A door closes, a door opens.' This is what he tells me.

He leaves me to wonder whether I have done just what he hoped I would do. I have noted down a tale as a legacy for his sons.

27

THEARY

Theary answers my phone call in a voice that is efficient and mature, yet still familiar. Then she realises who is calling. If I am in Cambodia I must come to stay in her house. Not able to stay all the time with her? Then at least a night. Yes? At least start with meeting her at the office, have lunch, have a rest in her house, have dinner, stay the night.

A little before lunch time I arrive by tuk-tuk at RACHA, Reproductive and Child Health Alliance, and am taken upstairs past a silk wall hanging, past floors of offices, to a long tiled corridor with doors on each side. I know the RACHA story: one hundred and fifty projects across almost all provinces in this country, safeguarding health and improving life for mothers and their babies. Theary has been executive director here for almost a decade, yet it seems that not so many years have passed since she was a new arrival from the refugee camp, unsure of everything, including where to find food to eat for her next meal.

Theary steps out from a door furthest from the staircase. 'Sister my sister.' She holds out her arms. We run along the corridor towards each other laughing. We meet and hug as we have done before, then stand apart to look at each other.

THEARY

She is wearing her dark hair shoulder length, softly curling and drawn back from her face. Her clothes are simple, tailored charcoal coloured trousers and a short-sleeved, V-neck cotton top. It is the colour of watermelon. She is slimmer than when I last saw her and more poised.

Theary introduces me to her colleagues. 'This woman has known me for a long time, like a sister,' she says. Her office is spacious. We draw up our chairs to a heavy table and, unexpectedly, she slides an album of wedding photos from a drawer.

'If you had been here just a little bit earlier you could have been at my wedding,' she says. We open the album. I'm wanting more than anything to hear about her new husband, not just to see the pictures. I guess it has been hard for any man to convince her to marry him; I know she has always been reluctant to shift her commitment away from the work she is doing.

As it happens Theary's husband is a leader with important international development projects in Central America. He seems to understand that she cannot leave behind this work of hers in Cambodia and is content that for now they will be together whenever they can.

I scan the album with its first pages showing a ceremony in the USA; her husband is American. Step by step I gain a picture of him. Theary is wearing a Western wedding gown with the addition of a crimson Cambodian silk sash around her waist. Her husband is dressed in formal Western clothes; so too are his family and friends clustered around the couple. We turn the pages to the Cambodian ceremonies; bride and groom are pictured in the series of traditional costumes, as is custom. 'He was very patient with it all,' she says.

We share news of old friends as Theary drives me through the traffic to her narrow triple-storey home in a quiet street. As she cooks our food and brings it to the table she asks about my writing and we talk about the past, about the time that she left the camp and went to Sydney, about the episode of my bleeding nose.

Next day we lunch and laugh with Mary, Theary's friend and mentor from border days. They came back into Cambodia together. Life was struggle for them both in those early days. Theary's experience on the border was an obstacle and not an asset then; now she is leading a staff of hundreds of development workers, medics and doctors trained in Phnom Penh.

$$\Omega$$

I sit on Theary's sofa, in my hand a glass of wine that an Australian volunteer has brought to this gathering. The conversation is about medical ethics. Those gathered at her home have qualified in different parts of the world, all are discussing the particular problems in Cambodia, where their profession, as they aim for best-practice, is constrained by power and corruption. Out-of-date medication from other countries is finding its way to clinics where poor people are treated. Patients are endangered, so too is the health system they have worked to develop. Theary and Nee are taking a lead in technical discussions that I appreciate but don't fully understand.

I had forgotten Nee's medical training, but Theary has not.

28

NEE

We drive to Kampong Cham, Nee and I, at 6.30 on a clear morning, enjoying the early light. Once we are away from the busy streets of Phnom Penh we talk together of recent protests, of the bloodshed and the arrests.

'Did you notice the protest on the airport road the other day?' he asks. I hadn't noticed, but I would like to hear about it. Displaced people whose land had been grabbed by officials were protesting. They had been helped to research carefully in preparation and had found that on one occasion Prime Minister Hun Sen had denounced land-grabbing. On their banners they had an image of the Prime Minister with his wife, the words he had spoken and the date he had spoken them. When armed military police surrounded them these protesters had asked, 'Are you against our Prime Minister?' Those who had come to harass them stepped back in confusion.

Today Nee will teach at a university, the first formal session for the first PhD group in Kampong Cham with a qualified Cambodian educating others who are entering into the protracted struggle of planning and completing a thesis. Those who can persevere with this effort will be among the thinkers and leaders needed by their country.

I settle back to enjoy this journey even though I had expected to take the direct road north to Battambang. It is a lengthy detour. Our route is edged with rice fields and small villages. I understand that Nee is wanting me to meet his students but as we drive he suggests that I might do some teaching.

'Together with you?' I am not ready to agree to teach unprepared to students I do not know.

'Yes, we can do it together.' The drive is long; we have time to plan.

We stop for breakfast in the sunshine, eat noodles and check preparations for the classes ahead. Nee reaches up to the rear-vision mirror of the car. Hooked to it is a grey-and-white striped necktie, neatly tied, ready for use on formal occasions. He exchanges his plastic thongs for shoes and socks.

As soon as we park in the university car park we are ushered into a tutorial room. The relaxed morning switches pace, as the doctoral candidates are eager. Nee gives them his total attention. He shifts his concentration from one to another of them: questioning, listening, and explaining. Each one's struggle to frame a research question is vitally important. Throughout the long morning the focus does not waver. Nee holds authority. These well-dressed students around the table may see him as shabby and battered by life, despite his effort of necktie and brown shoes, but they hold to his every word.

A professor whispers a request. I nod in agreement and he passes a message to masters-level students around the campus that they would be welcome to attend the afternoon session.

The doctoral candidates sit behind us on a platform, where I am the only woman. Students not able to fit into the large hall watch through the louvre windows. I am astounded at such enthusiasm. We teach together, with Nee taking the lead as we have done over and again in these years. Among the men and the monks down there in the hall there are young women. My words are for them. The sun is sinking as the day's teaching finishes.

It is dusk, then darkness, as we drive back to Phnom Penh with the longer journey to Battambang ahead. Nee maintains his fast-paced agenda by concentrating on one thing at a time. He is to teach the early Sunday morning class in a university in Battambang. When I agreed to this journey I had not understood that we would need to return to Phnom Penh before travelling north.

Phnom Penh's city lights glitter and bedazzle. There is a stark contrast at the outer limits of town. The gap between the places of the rich and the places of the poor is profound.

Highway Five is in darkness; the moon has not yet risen. Nee is driving, reaching the speed limit of sixty kilometres an hour when he can. The traffic which comes towards us is so dense and erratic that more often we edge forward with the speedometer reaching thirty or forty.

To stay awake we recall and tell stories. The road turns and the moon rises in front of us; it hangs as a thin crescent, faintly tinged with red. We reach Kampong Chhnang well past midnight, when no story is good enough to keep us from yawning. It is impossible to go further in safety. We take two rooms in a simple hotel for a few hours of sleep and set the alarms on our mobile phones.

This pace is, I realise with worry, routine for Nee.

$$\Omega$$

The car headlight carves a cone of light through the darkness. There is energy now in this pre-dawn time. Nee is telling me about a dream that is with him as he wakes each morning. He dreams of a farm, of a quiet life there. This image of 'the farm' is a peaceful beginning to the day.

'I've already bought two hectares of farmland and I've sunk a well.'
'What are you looking for?'
'Time. To think more deeply, to reflect, to write.'

I have heard this before, we have had similar conversations for years now; twice he has tried to give it shape. He spent a very brief spell in a monastery but the quietness he longed for was impossible as the monks came to him and asked him to teach them about development. Later there was a futile though initially joyous attempt to set up a farm in Pailin.

The fronds of the coconut palms trace feathery black against the first glow of dawn; they become soft deep green when lit by the headlights. We watch the sky change: salmon pink, amber, pearl grey. As darkness merges with morning on National Route Five he talks once more of the dream: a place of quietness away from his over-committed life, a place where his spirit will be strong.

There is now enough light to distinguish the flurry of the start of day. People from roadside villages are organising the day's work, loading pushcarts, sweeping, scattering water to settle the dust. Bicycles and motorbikes edge into the traffic flow. The sky becomes blue and it is 6.30. We pass a small roadside market where women squat beside laden baskets, arranging fruit and vegetables. Loud speakers boom popular romantic music; we are folded in a flurry of dust and the chanting of monks in the nearby pagoda.

Nee says, 'I want to prepare for the last part of my life.'
'What do you imagine?'

There will be a timber house of one room and a bathroom. Here he will be enclosed in silence and surrounded by growing things, the plants and the animals.

'Animals?'

'Yes, animals.' This, he is sure, will soon become a reality. 'As soon as there is a house and a generator I will be able to live there.'

I turn to look at him. Though his attention is still on the road, delight has spread across his face. He can see this farm as he wants it to be, as he says the words to describe it. The edge of the back fence and the two side fences will be closely planted with bananas. In the first year each plant will produce one bunch, in the second year two bunches and in the third four or five. Along the front fence there will be a particular kind of coconut palm yielding small sweet fruit. There is already a heap of compost for the planting. Mangoes and limes can be planted first, then beds prepared for vegetables. There will be small animals, and eventually a pond for fish-farming. 'In the early mornings, after tending to the farm, there will be time to think and to write.'

From time to time a motorbike veers in from the kerb. Close to villages Nee holds his hand on the car horn to remind the bike riders of cars on the road. The highway is familiar. He drives steadily while giving his attention to the rest of his life, 'the last part.'

'There will still be the chance to teach in the universities and to support village groups.' He is as clear about the shape of this as he is clear about the garden of the two-hectare block. The teaching will always be to enable people to think for themselves: illiterate village people, indigenous hill tribe people or PhD candidates.

'This is the way change happens,' he says. People become free, people find the courage to release themselves from oppression, once they begin to look at their lives and to seek answers. In the strengthening light Nee chooses words carefully.

'Remember when we read Paulo Friere. Try to discover the question that touches the lives of people. Then they begin to think critically. Step by step they understand what is happening.'

We are nearing Battambang now. 'Facebook is a way to ask questions. I'm not rich or politically powerful but many people in Cambodia and overseas keep contact with me. There will be good access to wi-fi in the farmhouse.' I listen and hope that all of this can happen. I fear, but do not say, that Nee's future is as unpredictable as that of Cambodia.

We have reached the edge of Battambang. Between Saturday morning and Sunday morning we have travelled close to six hundred kilometres. It is time for Nee to find the grey-and-white striped tie on the rear vision mirror and the shoes and socks under the driver's seat, and for me to reach for my bag.

Friends in Battambang wait for me.

29

BATTAMBANG

For a day and a night I have been celebrating Chinese New Year with Battambang friends who can claim a Chinese ancestor somewhere on the family tree. Never in earlier years have I heard talk of a Chinese ancestor but Chinese New Year is becoming fashionable as an extra holiday.

The women of the families have cooked the elaborate meal that is requisite for this occasion. They have observed the ritual of placing the gold coloured pouches laced with gunpowder one by one on an open fire. It is a noisy recall of the ancestors. I welcome the silence now.

Battambang town feels familiar even in the pre-dawn darkness. I recognise the mingled smell of tropical fruit, garbage, frangipani and steamed rice as I sit alone in a quiet place, a high flat rooftop with a chair and a small garden of green plants in pots.

It is a little before 5.30 in the morning. The old Battambang market, Phasar Nhat, with its clock stopped since Year Zero Khmer Rouge time, is below me in the starlight. When it is light I will walk across the bridge to Wat Kandal, 'the central wat', to meet Bob. The monks have not yet started chanting.

There is a pinpoint of light in the darkness below. Someone down in the market has lit a Chinese New Year fire in a tin bucket. The flames cast a glow on the market benches, the stools and the rafters. Staccato retorts slice through the silence and I smell the gunpowder.

As if the first lighting was a challenge another fire and yet another is lit. Rat tat-tat-tat-tat-tat-tat-tat below where I am sitting is followed by tat-tat-tat-tat-tat-tat from west, north and south. The sound is enough to awaken the dead. I try to think of the veneration that is intended, not the violent explosions that happen.

I recall a dark morning in Battambang town in 1992. I was sitting at a roadside table. It was this same brief time of tropical darkness turning to light. My hand steadied the steaming glass of dark coffee laced with sweetened condensed milk balanced on the tin table. A very young soldier with plastic thongs on his feet sat down beside me and rested his AK-47 and his hand-held rocket launcher beside my coffee. I knew that soon he would mount the back of a motorbike and head to battle. 'Yeay, the mosquitoes bit me last night,' he said as he rolled up his sleeve to show me the bites on his arm.

He was younger than Reaksa is now.

At first light I cross the bridge to Wat Kandal, to Bob's residence within the walls of the monks' place. It is a small Buddhist dwelling painted ochre yellow, its stone front steps leading to a patio that acts as classroom. Trees surround and shelter it, amplifying the peace, separating it from other buildings. In a recent era it was used as a torture centre; now Cambodians, many of them young, come here to learn about non-violence.

The patio is spacious, clean and airy though here and there the paint is peeling from the wall-plaster and some of the floor tiles are broken. The walls are papered in a patchwork of peace: hundreds of coloured posters, peace stickers, images, paintings and photographs.

BATTAMBANG

They have been sent here from friends and supporters from around the world.

There are quotes attributed to well-known and unknown peacemakers.

> We must find the courage to leave our temples and enter the temples of human experience, temples that are filled with suffering.
>
> Maha Ghosenanda

> Lead me from death of life,
> from falsehood to truth.
> Lead me from despair to hope,
> from fear to trust.
> Lead me from hate to love,
> from war to peace.
> Let peace fill our hearts, our world, our universe.
>
> Anon

> I mourn the loss of a thousand precious lives, but I will not rejoice in the death of one, not even an enemy. Returning hate for hate multiplies hate, adding deeper darkness to a night already devoid of stars. Darkness cannot drive out darkness: only light can do that. Hate cannot drive out hate: only love can do that.
>
> Martin Luther King, Jr.

WRITING FOR RAKSMEY

As I wait for Bob to return to this place where the walls speak of what he yearns to do, the monks sweep fallen leaves into mounds. They set them alight and I am ringed with smoke rising in the still air. I think of the smoking ceremony of Australian Aboriginal peoples. It is cleansing.

30

TOUERN

Touern wants me to stay in her house.

She takes me there on the motorbike. This journey is familiar; it is as if nothing has changed. We set out together in the evening after a gathering with Krom Akphiwat Phum. We cross the river on the bridge near Wat Kandal then enter the roundabout with the huge statue of the Battambang legend. We swerve around the triple-life-size dark man sitting scantily clothed on a dais with legs crossed, baton in hands, eyes blazing. The ancient Battambang legends stretch far back.

We travel south past the new university and the abandoned airport until the busy edge of town is left behind. The avenue of trees is familiar; the left turn to the side road is rough as it always was. The way in and out of the village where Touern has lived since she first brought me here is reached by motorbike, bicycle or walking. Her husband has died. He left the family home long ago, never able to recover from the three years, eight months, twenty days of the Pol Pot time. She wears a woven band of remembrance around her wrist.

A few precious fruit trees have been cut to allow for connection of power lines for the house. All else is the same. There is a glow of light inside and the sound of children. Touern holds the light of the motorbike steady so that I can see the ladder. I enter the house face first, a gradual arrival through the square entrance-hole cut in the living room floor, and am immediately surrounded: greeted and hugged by the sons, introduced to the wives, tugged at by their children.

Everyone is seated on the floor. The hammock tied from post to post still swings as it has for years; perhaps it is the same hammock. Whenever an adult or a child goes close to it they give it a push.

This small house, which was originally one room, now has three corners partitioned off to form tiny bedrooms: one for Touern, one for her first son, his wife and children, one for the second son, his wife and baby.

All of these people are together on the floor of the main room. One wife is breastfeeding her child, with her husband sitting beside her, his gaze fixed on them tenderly. His hair is cut short; it stands straight and dark around his head. I recall him sitting right there as a small boy with his hair standing dark and straight around his head.

Touern watches as I greet them all. I know that she is proud she reared them virtually alone; she ensured that they each had a good education, employment and, when the time came, a dignified and traditional marriage ceremony.

I watch the swinging hammock, fascinated. When there is a chance I edge around the room to look inside.

There is a baby so small that she makes no bump in the heavy folded blanket. Her head rests on a pillow edged with a pink satin frill and an applique of a pink dolphin. She has an orange coloured knitted hat. On her hands, which she holds near her face, are mitts like boxing gloves made of blue and white felt. The heavy blanket is tan coloured with a huge yellow and green sunflower. Her eyes are closed. The buzz of talk in the room does not disturb her at all.

TOUERN

Everybody has been waiting for me to meet this latest member of the family. Touern nuzzles lovingly against her, making gurgling sounds as I have seen her doing with her own babies years ago.

Ω

Touern still goes to the villages and sleeps among the people, listening, questioning, encouraging. Whatever is achieved the people are able to say, 'We did it ourselves.' She still chooses the poorest villages, stays day and night, guides the conversations that uncover hope so that village people dare to plan for a future. 'Help them to listen to the dreams of each other,' she says.

We talk into the night as we always did in this cupboard-like space that is her bedroom.

'What is the most important, Touern?'

'Love the people.'

'Are there some that you love most?'

Pause. 'I love them all.'

I remember that Tolstoy wrote, 'Everything I know I know only because I love.'

In the morning I watch Touern in action in her own village. Her energy does not waver. She draws people together without words. Sometimes I think that it happens mainly through that sideways look, the backward nod of her head, her eyes. It could never be described in a textbook of community development. She turns tension to laughter with an offhanded quip. That is who she is.

As we meet family after family in the village where she lives we pause to talk to everyone. In each household there is a grandchild or cluster of grandchildren being cared for while the parent is in

Thailand earning a wage that could never be earned in Cambodia. Touern's own daughter is a cleaner in a hospital there. Her baby is with her; the small daughter stays with Touern. This is the only way her daughter will ever be able to live independently, as she wants to do, in her own small house.

31

KROM

I return to the people of Krom Akphiwat Phum as I always do when in Battambang. I am expected of course: news travels fast in Cambodia. We sit together on the floor mat as we always have, though in the rented house that is now the base there are some tables and chairs. The veteran friends from the beginning want more than anything else to tell me of their lives and their families. I make sure that I have a chance to meet new members of the team. Times change and Krom Akphiwat Phum adjusts.

A young woman has recently been selected for a place among the twelve. She has graduated after four years of university studying community development and realising that she needs experience for the theory to make sense.

Those who have gained so much from two decades out in the villages worry about how they can pass on their experience. 'We are like old bamboo that needs to find new green shoots,' they say. The friendly give-and-take has not changed. We joke that Ean once said he would stay with this work until his hair was like the rough outside of a coconut. 'This is it. Your hair is like the outside of a coconut now.'

The practices and the vision of the original Krom can still be recognised, though for most of its twenty years Nee and Ka have not been involved. There is still a gender balance in the leadership: six men and six women. It is still about helping people to develop by any means possible, and watching over the development of village communities. The poorest are still listened to; their concerns mould the planning. The work has spread across many villages where the local people now manage these projects.

I read Krom's proposals and evaluations and sometimes meet with International NGOs who are considering whether to support them financially.

$$\Omega$$

An unexpected email appears in my inbox. An American friend from Site 2 days, the anthropologist Lindsay French, has kept contact with Krom during the years. She and her documentary-making husband, Peter O'Neill, have captured the story on camera. I follow the links to their site as they invite me to watch the film. I write to tell them that I am delighted with the way the spirit of the work has been depicted, but also mention my worry that the spirit being built in the villages could make the Krom and the village people a target. The rich, the powerful and the corrupt will retaliate as the poor dare to hope for a better life. Lindsay replies:

> I think the Krom themselves wonder how this will all work out. It is a risky business, to create hope. I am impressed with their truly dogged determination. They need some younger staff, though; they are getting tired. Unfortunately, very few younger people share their perspective, which has been forged through experiences nobody wants repeated. BUT at least they – the younger people – can and should know about these experiences. This is where your storytelling comes in.

This time, as always, the warmth of the welcome when I return to Krom becomes a lively party. But the serious questions remain.

32

PEOU AND THALIKA

When the music of the Krom party has finished and the mat rolled back into place, when darkness is coming and the women of the team should leave for home before nightfall, when we have tidied away the scraps of an impromptu meal, Thalika stays back to talk to me.

For more than a decade I have watched Thalika's loneliness. He continued to work but the man who had amazed us with his dancing, who had charmed the Australian TV crews, who had enough compassion to protect a quadriplegic brother and a young family, seemed to have disappeared. Now I enquire about Peou.

I knew Peou for a long time. She married young, as Thalika did. She had children who had grown up and made their way in the world, as Thalika's did. When I was first told of her love for Thalika and his love for her I was glad of their happiness. They studied similar courses at university; both have experienced village life and understand it. They shared the same passion for giving dignity back to simple people, whose suffering they could comprehend. Peou works with women who have suffered violence; she is as vivacious as Thalika is reserved.

Now while there is the chance to talk with Thalika alone I ask about Peou's health. Not long ago I arrived at their house to find Peou ill; she was diagnosed as having throat cancer and needing chemotherapy. It was not available in Cambodia. Thalika was preparing to take her to Vietnam for treatment. Worry etched one more layer of lines on Thalika's face.

The next time I came they were not in Battambang. Now Thalika urges me to come to stay with them.

Ω

I wait at the river edge of Street One for Thalika to come on his motorbike to take me to his home.

The 'new' house of Thalika and Peou is at the end of a row of simple houses in a Battambang back street. Peou has lived in something far more elaborate; Thalika has earned a steady salary and has skills that should enable a comfortable life. But the cancer treatment was very expensive.

Peou is waiting at the doorway as we take off our helmets and our shoes before stooping to enter the cooler interior. She hugs me and says 'I'm so happy.' We sit together on the mat and Peou pours soft drinks while we talk of some part-time study that Thalika is doing at a local university.

I look around in this ground-level room. Bedding is stacked at the edge of the mat where we sit. The side wall is set for cooking and dishwashing. There are books. Though I know that Thalika's dignity can mask a great deal of worry I begin to feel reassured. They are not talking of cancer.

After we have finished our drinks Thalika disappears to a house across the road. Peou and I are tidying away the glasses when he returns with a baby girl in his arms. 'She's so beautiful,' I say. At last Thalika smiles. 'She's ours.' The little girl is called Amara. 'It means

Queen of Heaven,' says Peou who became pregnant soon after her last chemotherapy treatment.

Amara is walking at 11 months old, tiny enough to walk under a table, steady on her feet. She will not take her eyes away from Thalika and should he move towards his motorbike she drops to her knees and crawls after him. Her crawling is faster than her walking. Her father dotes on her and she doesn't want him out of her sight.

This evening and every evening Peou and Thalika spread a broad sleeping mat across the downstairs room of their house, set up a giant sleeping net and settle on cushions under the net as Amara quietens into sleep. They say, and I believe, that though they have few possessions they are completely happy.

I sleep in the attic room upstairs.

In dappled sunshine at the doorway of their house we share breakfast of Cambodian bread and coffee. Amara is playing with some soft toys, showing them to each of us, arranging them along a bench.

Thalika and I look at the way his story is written. He remembers the sadness of so many years and he talks of the happiness now. We remember stories of Krom Akphiwat Phum. Though a new generation may need to take Krom forward in a different manner suited for a new time, Thalika hopes that the new way would continue to be based on staying close to the people of the village, listening to them, earning their trust through nights and days spent there, supporting the natural leaders from among the people and always including the poorest. We talk about the university-educated young woman who has joined the team. Thalika and other veterans of the work at Krom keep talking about the best ways of passing on their experience while there is still time. They are thinking of pairing to take a half salary each so that a young person could be employed on a full salary.

'What is it that has kept the spirit of Krom strong?'

Peou joins the conversation. She tells me of her work in the Banteay Srei safe house for women who dare to take their husband to court for violence.

'Sometimes I wonder whether the spirit of Banteay Srei is strong because of what you have learned through your own suffering.' I am thinking out loud, not intending to pry.

There is silence; even Amara is alert to it. Then Peou tells of the time her hands were tied behind her back as she watched her brother tortured with his hands behind his back and his face in the dust. She did not see him again. She has never stopped working for women who suffer.

33

PHALY AND SOEUN

In Battambang I hear the news about Phaly. Nee is in Rattinakiri. I phone him and we both return to Phnom Penh.

We come to the orphanage hurriedly in the night: Nee, his sons and me. Soeun stands in the darkness of the roadside waiting for us. He wraps his arms around each of us in turn. 'It was a road accident,' he says. 'We did everything we could to save her. We did everything we could to save her. She died. Phaly died.' He leads us to the reception area of the orphanage.

The pathway through the garden to the door of the Future Light Orphanage is brightly lit, edged with trees and flowers. 'Of course,' Nee says softly, 'We knew that for Phaly there would be beautiful flowers and plants in pots.' We enter through glass doors. A large coloured image of Phaly's face and silk clad shoulders dominates a lofty space; the frame is wreathed in flowers. Soeun watches as we look at it. 'Recent,' he says. 'A recent picture.' She looks serene and gracious, younger than her seventy-four years, her face giving no hint of the life she has lived.

The table below Phaly's image is draped in silk; it holds an ornately patterned china urn. In front of this is a gilded tray holding Phaly's perfumes, in front of that another tray holds her cosmetics. Furthest from the urn is a plate of her favourite food. The shrine is decked with flowers and is tended by Phaly's daughter, together with a woman who has worked with her since the long-ago KPDR. Beside the shrine on a table of its own is a box containing a book in which visitors are invited to write a message. I write for the four of us and then for Claudia in Switzerland, Lud in Africa, and Mary in Australia. They would want to be here.

Nee, his sons and I pay our respects one by one.

Soeun guides us around the five hectares of the orphanage. He shows us the first small packet of land that Phaly's mother gave when they returned from Site 2. The trees, which he immediately planted, form a huge avenue now. We walk through a tunnel roofed in leaves.

Young women who are finishing their studies while still living in the orphanage cluster around me; they show me the separate dormitory blocks for boys and girls, the computer classroom and the language classroom where there are evening classes after a day spent in local primary or secondary schools. They show me the lake where a group of young men are, even at this time of night, discussing the technique of breeding fish for sale. The boys join us, making sure that we see the bicycle shed. It is large enough to hold a bike for each of the two hundred young people in the orphanage.

Nee walks behind, listening as Soeun talks to him. The two men bend their heads towards each other as they walk in and out of patches of light from the classrooms and dormitories. Soeun's grief soaks into us all. As he walks us back to our car he invites me to share in the orphanage memorial ritual for Phaly. It will be held on the water where the Mekong River merges with the Tonle Sap, a traditional place for scattering ashes.

$$\Omega$$

PHALY AND SOEUN

In the hot late-afternoon sun Thero talks on my mobile phone to my bewildered tuk-tuk driver, guiding him between a bank of buses parked along the kerbside close to where the children from the orphanage are boarding boats. I said goodbye to Phaly's son twenty years ago when he was very young. Now we meet in tears.

Soeun is silent and formal. All two-hundred children are being led down the steps to boats tied to the quay. I climb down to the water surrounded by this quiet throng.

The orphans, their carers, some young people who grew up in the orphanage and have returned, as well as a few friends of the family, all are respectfully quiet. Two large boats have been hired. We leave the jetty, the bustle of Phnom Penh recedes, we stand in silence at the rails. Thero and Soeun distribute a long-stemmed lotus flower to each of us.

We reach the point where the Tonle Sap and the Mekong merge. Soeun leads me to the bow of our boat to stand between himself and Thero, to pray silently, then aloud and, one after the other, cast our flowers into the water. Everyone on both boats follows. Lotus flowers swirl in eddies on the merging streams.

The brief twilight ends; strings of party lights looped around the decks of the boats are switched on, and the mood changes. Most of the children have never been on a boat before. Lights reflect on the water, rippling in patterns. Excited boys and girls call from boat to boat. Tables and chairs are brought on to the decks and food is served, warm rice and as many delicacies as Phaly would have wanted. Children and adults tell stories of her life and begin to laugh.

I sit with Thero and Soeun. Thero is showing me images on his iPhone as he tells me of his mother's accident. Phaly had been working in Ratanakiri; the orphanage had a base there. Since the journey was a long one there were two drivers. On the road between Ratanakiri and Kampong Cham the less experienced driver was taking his turn. Phaly was sitting in the back seat working on her laptop, without her seatbelt fastened. When the car swerved from the road and overturned nobody else was injured but it was immediately evident that Phaly's injuries were grave.

Thero is consoled by the thought that his mother was never left alone during the eighteen days between her accident and her death. When Phaly was brought to Phnom Penh he had her transferred to the hospital with a reputation for being the best in this city. She was there for a few days when this 'best hospital' closed to Cambodians because the ASEAN Summit meeting was about to begin. It was made ready for international delegates who might need it. Thero then chartered a plane to bring his mother to the best hospital he could find in Bangkok but she was bleeding internally and doctors said that nothing could be done. She died there thirteen days later. Thero recalls it day by day and shows me the images of Phaly lying in her bed.

34

RAKSMEY

I meet Raksmey in Proan Pra on the outskirts of Phnom Penh, across the river in the distinctly unstylish south-west. A short time ago this was scarcely more than a mass of shanties housing impoverished fishing families who had come up the river from Vietnam and were scorned by Cambodians in the better parts of town. Now property developers are throwing up rows of houses, all attached: house after house opening straight on to the street, identical in style and colour, each with a tiny backyard.

Nee has borrowed money to buy a house that he and his two sons can call home. Previously they have shared each place they have lived with many cousins from the countryside coming to the city to study. Nee worked to support nieces and nephews until they finished or dropped out of their courses. Now there is a home for his sons and himself.

Raksmey and his brother are old enough to be independent and are securely housed. Nee has earned enough money to give them the education he judged to be the best in Cambodia. The family is entering a new phase.

Proan Pra is a long way from Raksmey's university, his work and his friends. He leaves on his motor bike while the morning is still dark and crosses the most congested streets before the build-up of vehicles reaches its peak. He stops to eat breakfast where he knows the food will be cheap and good, then spends the morning as a volunteer at the Cambodian Development Resource Institute. His university lectures are in the afternoon. In the evening he eats and studies with his friends and returns home when it is time to sleep.

He asks for a copy of the stories I have written in my draft manuscript, saying that Sunday will be a good time for reading it. I have already left Phnom Penh when my mobile phone rings. It is Raksmey, he has been reading. 'You did this for me. Thank you. It is what I needed to know.'

Then, since we often talk together about literature he says, 'I like your use of irony. I'm reading Dickens and Pearl Buck. There is something similar.' I laugh.

35

RATANAKIRI

Nee squats in the dust as a cluster of the hill-tribe people of Ratanakiri, young and old, men and women, settle around him. He uses few words. He has been working with groups like this for a long time. The way he leads them is unobtrusive and relaxed.

What are they noticing?

Only two years ago this place where they meet was dense forest, now their land has been 'grabbed' and Vietnamese businessmen have been granted a ninety-nine-year lease. Their forest is cleared, the wild animals have disappeared, the giant logs have been carted away on trucks. Politicians and business-men have become very rich. It is now a rubber plantation.

What do they hear when they listen to the talk of other local people? The discussion divides into language groups; it is staccato, full of energy. Khmer is not their first language. These people speak ancient languages.

I look around. We are surrounded by rubber tree saplings at the edge of the plantation. The only other vegetation is on a tiny garden block close to a house beside the dirt road. A slight breeze, welcome in the heat, ruffles the leaves of a lone mango tree where hens scratch the denuded earth. A truck skids along the road, raising more dust, caking it in the cracks of our lips, spreading grit on our teeth. It settles into the folds of skin and clothes. We blink the sting from our eyes.

Women and men from the neighbourhood draw closer to join in conversation. They are united in their urgent desire to 'do something'.

A father holds his bike still and offers his opinion. An old woman comes; there are gaps in her mouth where teeth once were. Her sarong is worn to holes, her krama is knotted around her head, covering her hair and shading her face. A middle-aged woman with glossy black hair knotted at the nape of her neck speaks with few words; her quiet authority is enough to still the crowd. A dark, thin, restless young activist is stirred by his own words.

In each lull Nee, in a gentler voice, poses one more question.

None of these people have been offered employment in the rubber plantation which replaces their forest. They have lived from their forest. What do they worry about most?

They grieve that their culture is lost.

While they speak in local languages Nee sits with me on the ground. 'This may be the most dangerous time. More and more poor people have begun to claim their dignity. They are ready to protest, to die.' They are powerless and ripe to be stirred to rage. 'I can understand anger,' he says. 'Some activists deliberately use the anger. But it is better to go slowly. There has to be a way of acting that is well-planned and coordinated, that avoids bloodshed. There has been too much blood.' He will give them whatever time it takes to plan, for leadership to be nurtured.

Nee knows that this is delicate. The military police are primed to fire randomly whenever there might be the slightest sign of antagonism. Only this week there have been more deaths. 'Angry resistance would be like feeding a crocodile,' he says. He is working so that those who have been dispossessed will be freed to think, not simply roused to react.

Back at his laptop in Ratanakiri town Nee networks to strengthen his international links. There is a glimmer of hope. Two of the global banks providing loans to the rubber companies are considering their codes of ethics.

36

IENG SARY AND KIEU SAMPHAN

I prepare to leave for Australia. Theary invites me to one more meal before I go. I sit at her table with Raksmey and Reaksa on my left, Nee and Theary on my right.

Nee has a message on his mobile phone. There is a rumour that Ieng Sary, the deputy to Pol Pot, has died. He checks contacts for confirmation and finds that the rumour is correct. Ieng Sary has died in hospital, surrounded by family. The three defendants still awaiting trial in the Khmer Rouge Tribunal are Ieng Sary's wife, Ieng Thirith, who has been declared unfit to stand trial because of dementia, Nuon Chea and Khieu Samphan. Nuon Chea is also old and sick.

I look towards Raksmey and Reaksa. If they are listening this is a conversation they might remember to tell their grandchildren. Reaksa is nevertheless more interested in the distinctly Khmer apartment Theary has fashioned: carvings, pictures and wall hangings produced by Cambodian artists and craftspeople, the heavy Cambodian-timber dresser displaying local pottery and ceramics decorated with traditional designs. He appreciates it all and wants to talk to me about it.

Theary, the attentive hostess, offers each of us the fish and the thick beef soup she has chosen and prepared, then returns to the conversation with Nee about the news of the day. The Extraordinary Chamber in the Courts of Cambodia was not constituted in time to try Pol Pot. He died in Khmer Rouge territory back in 1998. Almost two million people are believed to have perished between 1975 and 1979; the only person whose trial has been completed is Duch.

I know that if I join this conversation Reaksa and Raksmey will stay wordless; Theary's dinner table is more formal than Nee's sons are used to. Reaksa is fascinated with the light fitting. 'Look at this Yeay. It is energy efficient.' He is hoping that when there is enough money he will be able to organise tradespeople to renovate his father's house, and is gathering ideas.

Theary and Nee are talking of Khieu Samphan as he was when a young lecturer at the University in Phnom Penh. They have always heard that he was a man who lived simply, travelled by bicycle, cared about the poor. They have sympathy for him. He gained his PhD in Paris. He was a government minister in Sihanouk's time. He made the cause of the poor his cause and suffered for this. There is a story about the young Khieu Samphan angering Sihanouk by taking a stand with destitute workers in Battambang province; though a cabinet minister in Sihanouk's government he was stripped naked and cast out on to the Phnom Penh streets. This might catch Reaksa's attention; I look sideways to him. Raksmey is already listening.

In the early '70s Khieu Samphan emerged as a senior member of the Khmer Rouge. Is he 'Mr Clean', ignorant of what the regime was doing? Nee seems to be saying that Khieu Samphan is a gracious old man, 'eighty-one years old.' He chose to live quietly in Palin while he awaited trial. No longer a member of the Khmer Rouge, he consistently asserts that his role was limited, that he was kept away from decision-making and was used as a figurehead.

A Battambang university where Nee is lecturing arranged for him to spend an evening with Khieu Samphan at his house near the border of Thailand. They talked together into the night, these two Cambodians with their overseas doctorates. Khieu Samphan said that during the Khmer Rouge time his role was simply to watch over Sihanouk and eventually to prevent him being taken hostage by the Vietnamese. Just before the fall of Phnom Penh he protected Sihanouk and ensured that he was able to cross through to Thailand and so find refuge in China. Nee tried to draw Samphan to comment on the atrocities committed by the Khmer Rouge, but failed.

$$\Omega$$

The next morning, as I wait at Pochentong Airport for my flight from Phnom Penh to Singapore to Melbourne, I buy the international and Cambodian newspapers. Ieng Sary's death is reported in both. His family will take him from the Phnom Penh hospital to his home province to honour him with dignified ceremonies of mourning.

The Phnom Penh Post also reports:

> Speaking at an inauguration ceremony at Preah Sihamoni Reachea Buddhist University in Phnom Penh's Chamkarmon district yesterday, Hun Sen said that the attempts of the first four people – King Norodom Sihamoni, Queen Mother Norodom Monineath and two chief monks – had failed because candles had gone out and portions of the pyre had failed to ignite.
>
> After they tried, Hun Sen said, he had stepped in. The flames caught and spread.

IENG SARY AND KIEU SAMPHAN

I read that the 'temporary crematorium', which cost one million American dollars to construct, has been taken down, and the site is cleared.

I check my email using the airport wi-fi. There is one from Thero. He read what I wrote about his family; he would like to see it published, even as excerpts in the newspaper. He could do something about it; his profession is publishing. I reply that I wrote it for the family; it will be there for his young twins when they are old enough to understand it. I say that it would need a lot more work before publication. He replies that he understands and respects this.

My flight to Singapore is called. My travel documents are ready: arrival February 4th 2013, departure March 15th 2013.

37

STRUGGLES AND TENSIONS

In 2013 it is election year, in both Cambodia and Australia, a crucial year with tension mounting in both countries. Through email and Skype with Cambodian friends, and through reading Cambodian newspapers, I am alert to happenings there.

I read the Cambodia Daily and the Phnom Penh Post to follow the progress of the Extraordinary Chamber in the Courts of Cambodia. Anta Guisse, Kong Sam Onn and Arthur Vercken, defence lawyers for Khieu Samphan, are protesting perceived violations of its client's rights:

> It is now obvious that the dice are loaded. In its "race against death" conducted in the guise of a criminal trial, the Chamber has never been interested in what the Defense has had to say. Regularly cutting the microphones of the Defense lawyers and sanctioning those who protest is nothing other than the visible tip of the iceberg.

On 28 July, after heated political rallies and, seemingly, mass support for the opposition, Cambodians vote in the national election.

Nee phones his sons, who have both been cruising on motorbikes around the polling booths and are enthusiastically predicting a win

STRUGGLES AND TENSIONS

for the opposition. Their father tells them to return home immediately before the bridge is blockaded.

That afternoon there is lockdown in the city. People queue to withdraw their money from ATMs and petrol stations sell out of fuel.

The National Election Commission announces provisional results. Hun Sen's party, the CPP, will hold sixty-eight seats and the opposition CNRP fifty-five seats. The opposition leader, Sam Rainsy, calls for peaceful protest. He alleges electoral fraud orchestrated by the ruling party. One thousand protesters camp in Freedom Park and twenty thousand join street protests in Phnom Penh and provincial capitals. Monks in their saffron robes are strongly represented among the protesters. I watch a Radio Free Asia film clip showing a monk attempting self-immolation on a dais at a rally. He drenches himself with fuel. Others on the platform wrestle with him and prevent him from setting himself alight.

Ka sends me an email. 'This cruel man must not be permitted to rule Cambodia forever.' He is passionate about one thing now. Change must begin at the local level.

On 19 September Hun Sen is once more named as Prime Minister, extending his twenty-eight-year term for another five years. Parliament convenes. The fifty-five recently elected opposition members refuse to take up their seats.

$$\Omega$$

Australia's political struggles leave some of my Cambodian friends bemused. Kevin Rudd deposed Prime Minister Julia Gillard, 'and they were both alive next morning!' they say.

WRITING FOR RAKSMEY

On a wintery day I do the Australian housework: vacuum the rug, empty the compost, defrost the freezer. Refugees and asylum seekers are desperately trying to reach Australia. There are reports of boats. There are reports of drownings at sea. Australians are told, again and again, that seeking refuge is illegal. There are images of the overcrowded detention centres holding men, women and children behind secure fences as if they are criminals.

At night in the border camp I sometimes stayed among those who were detained behind the barbed wire. In this crowded place every man, woman and child was silently alert. A baby might cry, someone might mutter in sleep. Should there be a sinister sound, a thud or a scream, there was a simultaneous intake of breath. Everyone in this place was forever vigilant. I have heard the fear of those who have been afraid too long.

I stand at the kitchen window watching the drizzle of rain on the apple tree, needing to prepare a meal but thinking of Cambodia. News drifts from the radio. Our Prime Minister has just announced that nobody who comes by boat seeking safety will ever be settled in Australia. They will be processed offshore. The Papua New Guinea solution will be added to the Nauru solution. They will never find safety here. They don't exist for us.

I have seen too much suffering. Now I am stilled by feelings in a way I cannot name. Is it grief? Grief for Cambodia? Or shame? For Australia?

I think of the stories on the hard drive of my computer. They have served their purpose for Cambodian friends. Perhaps they could be useful in helping Australians to understand the choices made by ordinary people in truly terrible circumstances. The stories are not mine. I am considering what publishing them might mean for the Cambodians.

One memory focuses my reflection. It was 1998 in Battambang when, as I remember it, we were bunched around a black-and-white TV linked to a generator: Touern, Thalika, Nee and me. We saw destruction in Omagh, in Northern Ireland. Irish against Irish. There were broken buildings and bodies in the street. 'We could volunteer to help those people,' Nee said. 'We know what it is like.' There was a huddle of talk. They were confident then that the life they had lived had value for others who suffer.

During the night memories converge.

Night is becoming day. Purple-grey cloud has piled on the horizon; above it the sky changes from indigo, through aquamarine, to an expanse of clear pale blue. A fine crescent moon hangs high above the cloud. I know what I must do.

Next January I will be back in Cambodia. I will ask Cambodian friends whether I should try to have their stories published in Australia.

This has become as clear as that crescent moon on its back in the morning sky.

38

2014

On January 3rd, a short time before my plane lands in Pochentong Airport, military police armed with assault rifles open fire on several hundred workers demonstrating during a nation-wide strike for a just wage. At least four of the protesters or bystanders are dead and many more injured. One young man lying on the road bleeding from the head is not seen again. Nearby clinics are told to close their door against the injured. More than twenty are arrested and held without trial.

On the first day of my return Reaksa shows me a YouTube video of a Phnom Penh protest: a bank of military police, helmeted, booted, holding a body shield in one hand and a baton or AK-47 in the other, are advancing step by step towards unarmed protesters with placards, many without shoes. The dead lie in blood. The arrested, women and men together, lie face down on the road with hands tied behind their backs.

We talk through the afternoon and evening about the cost of struggling against oppression: of exploited garment workers, of families left homeless after their land has been grabbed by officials who will grow rich from its sale.

Reaksa sets up his laptop so that we can watch the film 'The Lady' together. 'You will see', he says. 'It will help you to understand about politics in Cambodia.' He needs me to see Aung San Suu Kyi's courage and the way she was ready to suffer for the sake of poor people of her country, Burma, now Myanmar. I remark on the way she believed that there was a seed of good in everyone. Reaksa is more interested in the scene where soldiers raised their guns and Aung San Suu Kyi walked without flinching towards them. 'This is it. Look at her. Nothing to fear but fear itself.' He has not yet known fear. 'Is it easier anywhere?' he asks. 'Could the UN give protection? Do people in other parts of the world care about what happens to us here?'

'Write my story, use my name,' he says. 'I would like it to be published.'

I shake my head. 'Think about this for a few days. Your friends might read it.'

He shakes his head. 'They won't read something like this until they are about thirty.'

He laughs and his mood changes. Reaksa is light-hearted now; he remembers his childhood. Spontaneously he begins to sing: he can hold a tune just as his mother could. He laughs and sings, 'Row, row, row your boat'; then, 'Incy wincy spider'.

We are both singing and making the shapes with our hands. 'Out came the sunshine and dried up all the rain, then incy wincy spider climbed the spout again.'

For a moment I think that he has remembered songs I sang to him and games that made him laugh before he could talk. 'Where did you learn these things?'

'On TV. Playschool.'

'Ah. Yes'

'This little piggy went to market', he says.

'Kookaburra sits on an old gum tree', I sing.

'Yes, yes.' We sing together, still singing on the motorbike as we set out to meet Raksmey.

39

KA

I sit in the bus to Battambang, thinking of this outbreak of violence and linking it to the dramatic change that seems to have happened in Ka since we last met. I read again what I wrote eleven months ago after talking to Ka and his sister.

$$\Omega$$

Ka insisted on taking me to breakfast, instructing me to wait for him close to the Independence Monument. I waited by the kerbside. A car with dark windows drew up beside me, the back door behind the driver opened and Ka and Lum Aung invited me to climb in beside them. Brother and sister both seemed strangely subdued as we drove to a Chinese restaurant in a fashionable street. This was not what I had expected; it was a while since I had seen them.

Ka talked soberly about his life. He has worked for the Mekong River Commission, the United Nations Development Program, the Asia Development Bank, the World Bank, and various INGOs and government ministries. He has managed to try everything that an aspiring and capable Cambodian would want to do yet he was disgruntled. I struggled to adjust to his air of regret.

This was not the Ka I remembered: Ka who came to my door in the long ago days of Krom Akphiwat Phum battered and bruised from a motorbike accident and announcing through laughter, 'I hit a hole and the bike stayed there. I flew like a bird and landed like a frog.' There was no laughter in the Chinese restaurant that morning. He sat slumped. This was a different hole, more difficult to laugh off. Over the years I had not noticed the gradual transformation. Now I saw it clearly.

Ka's hair no longer spiked around his head in a crew cut. It was tamed, parted and smoothed down in a traditional cut of short back and sides. He was neatly dressed in business clothes. Even his speech was formal.

Lum Aung finished ordering food then claimed my attention. She seemed to have planned what she needed to tell me. Much of it I knew already. 'After the coup of 1997 I continued in parliament serving three full terms of five years each. Three mandates. I chaired multi-party commissions. At the second and third election fewer and fewer FUNCINPEC members were elected.' At the fourth election she declined to stand.

I asked her then whether she had an opinion about the coming election. Her lips pressed together in her familiar gesture of determination. 'You remember Mu Sochua? Yes? Did you know she is a leader in the new coalition the Cambodian National Rescue Party? Yes? Sochua has urged me to consider re-entering the campaign to represent Battambang once more.'

I could understand this; few Cambodian women have had her experience. 'What did you say?'

'I said that I no longer believe that working for a political party is a way to assist the poorest of the women in rural Cambodia.'

While we stirred our expensive noodles that morning Lum Aung and Ka talked together about what they had failed to do; they talked of the barriers of corruption and nepotism. They had hoped, each in their own way, to influence events as their father's and their grandfather's generation did. They had wanted to make life better for those who suffer most. They told me that they could see nothing for their efforts.

$$\Omega$$

The bus is nearing Battambang; it is time to stop thinking of the Ka of last year and to meet the man who emailed me after the election. Passengers who live at the edge of town climb down stiffly from the bus, their luggage zipped into battered striped bags. At the central bus depot motor-dup drivers shout in unison and jostle for passengers. I don't need a motor-dup. Ka will be here expecting me. I wonder what to expect of him.

He arrives on a motorbike in minutes, wearing faded tee-shirt and shapeless jeans gathered at his hips with a leather belt. He bristles with energy as he takes my bag and guides me to a small drinks kiosk; it is without customers until we come. Ka orders a Coke and I a café duc doco, the strong local coffee with sweetened condensed milk.

We are close to Street Onc, where we met so many years ago.

I lean on the tin table and listen. The Ka who took me to a good restaurant in the black car with a driver, seen last year, has disappeared. The old Ka is back.

'What changed you?' I ask, remembering his earlier hopes and recent depression.

He shakes his head. During the years he saw too much corruption. He saw degradation of the natural resources of the country. The brutal suppression of public protest was the final jolt, cutting through lethargy and forcing him to weigh the choices he had made. 'It is the people who are poor who always suffer,' he says.

KA

Ka knows that I am writing. I have a draft of the manuscript and have marked the pages that mention his story, those that he would need to know about. He takes it eagerly; he will go straight back to Tean Tor, take a dipper shower and start reading.

Ω

As we set out for breakfast Ka says he has read for a long time in the night. I am on the back of the motorbike while he talks without waiting to reach the breakfast place he has chosen. The wind is in our faces; he is calling over his shoulder that there are two things that I need to adjust in my draft. In one place I had written Highway Ten; what I was writing about really happened on Highway Five. With regard to the incident of Sihanouk's officers there is one thing I should add to make it clearer. After Lon Nol's coup all of those officers had to belong to Lon Nol. He must have read much further than the pages I marked! 'What about the parts about yourself Ka?' I shout through the wind. He shouts back, 'They are correct.'

We eat our Chinese noodle soup hastily; the main thing this morning is to talk. We are very close here to his old family home. We passed it dusty and deserted. 'My God,' he says. 'My village was a calm and pretty place. It has become a beer garden.' Because the dusty new road to Pailin cuts close to the poles of the grand old house and heavy traffic rocks it day and night, he will not live there. He sleeps on the floor of the Tean Thor office.

Regret has given way to a sense of purpose in his life. He begins to talk about his father, a professional forester who urged him to study hard, to learn French, to prepare for a forestry degree in French. The Khmer Rouge changed all that. 'In the medical base during the fighting near the border I heard the terrible crying of the widows and of the ones with their limbs amputated. Poor people.'

From the Site 2 camp he had the chance to study in the Philippines. 'Those months changed my life,' he says. He has returned to his early vision, his energy for helping the poor in their struggle for justice. He says that his heart is full of pity for people who suffer so much. 'I have often tried to not think like that.' His eyes become red and wet. There is a tiny box of paper tissue in the middle of the table. Ka reaches with both hands and holds squares of tissue to each eye, blotting and ignoring as if those eyes did not belong to him he keeps talking without pause. 'Your life changes, you can't walk away.'

As we ride back to the office of Tean Thor I lean my helmeted head towards his to catch the words through the wind. 'Our OSB plan was right,' he says. 'Go to the village. Look. Listen. There are respected people there. They can be leaders.'

We are sit on benches in the Tean Thor office now, our helmets on the table between us. 'Local leadership ought not be appointed from the top, from levels of government,' he says. He tells of a time when he was in a meeting of around five-hundred top people where 'decentralisation' was being announced as a policy. It was explained that the government would appoint leaders for committees in the communes and districts and villages. 'This is what they called decentralisation!' He shakes his head and says that Hun Sen's party has not loosened its control of appointments down to the village level. In most places even the village leader is appointed through the CPP.

His hands make fists on the table. 'In this big public meeting I said, "bullshit".' No need to blot his eyes with tissue now. 'Bullshit! There is no place for national politics at the local level. This is bullshit. The people who live in a particular place know who really cares about them. At the local level let respected local people lead and let there be no domination by political parties.'

Tien Thor, which can be translated as 'Acts of Compassion', uses a small wooden house built on a cement floor for its office. There is one room large enough for a meeting of four or five people, a small room where one person could work alone and a bathroom with squat toilet and dipper shower. At night Ka sleeps in the meeting room. He has a laptop for setting up a forward plan for Tean Thor: his experience in international organisations has given him the skills to do this well.

I sit at the table in the cool inside space while Ka now stands in the doorway as he talks, the glare of the outside sun at his back.

'Awaken, educate, organise, and the people will have power,' he says. 'Rural people may be uneducated but they are clever.'

I listen through the morning. Ka reaches for his laptop and shows me photos of retaliation from armed military police against an unarmed demonstration. 'They are brave in facing the great dangers of standing for their rights but the repression against them is brutal.' Ka is shaking his head. 'When there is sacrifice of life who will care for the children of these families?' He shows me pictures of bloodied bodies and those who are arrested lying face down in the dirt.

Someone from Krom Akphiwat Phum telephones. It is midday already. Time for me to meet with the Krom team.

Ka has a last word. 'Society is falling apart again,' he says. 'You can do nothing without commitment.'

I remember the generations of the Ka family and the commitment they made as they lived in that house with sturdy poles set among trees. They knew how to make a difference for Battambang town and province. Things were clearer then.

40

LUM AUNG

Lum Aung comes to the doorway of her Phnom Penh home to greet me. As she stands holding the tin security gate open for me it seems that in less than a year since we last met she has grown smaller and frailer. Once inside I ask about her health. She has problems with fluctuating blood pressure and with her heart. She is over sixty years old now and is amazed that I am so much older and still healthy.

When the conversation turns to politics I forget my first impression of frailty. She is lively and forceful. She hopes that the international community will create the pressure to force a re-election. She is sure that the Cambodian National Rescue Party, the new coalition, is able to maintain a strong stance, having learned from what happened when FUNCINPEC had agreed to a coalition with Hun Sen. The fifty five elected members are still pledging not to sit in parliament until the electoral discrepancies have been investigated. They hope for a new election with close international monitoring. Lum Aung says that the next step should be huge demonstrations in Cambodia and in the Cambodian diaspora throughout the world.

As she sits on the bench by my side I notice that her earnest face has no lines of worry. We laugh together at the memory of that jar of face cream that she packed in her bag at the start of her political career. 'I am not a public person any more. For five years now I have not had to talk on radio or to newspapers. I am not afraid to criticise what I know is wrong. If I was still a public person the things that I must say would bring danger to some of my family. The situation is more frightening now than it ever was before. But I am not a public person so I can say what I like without being afraid of bringing suffering to my family and to Tien Thor.'

I say that I am worried that if I write about Ka's views this might cause trouble to him or to the family. 'Say what is true,' she says; 'Don't worry.'

A Cambodian proverb is passing around: 'Real gold is not afraid of fire.'

41

PROAN PRA

The Meas family home is my Phnom Penh base for this 2014 time in Cambodia. Nee's two sons want me to stay with them rather than in the small city guest house I had chosen. They say they need to be sure I am safe when I go to the city for a meeting or to the bus station for Battambang journeys. 'Just don't trust anyone else,' says Reaksa.

This house in the Proan Pra area of the city has space for the three of us. At the front there is a tiled main room. Neighbours in identical houses use this as a safe place for a car, as the metal security grill is wide enough to allow a vehicle to be driven in from the street. Since nobody in this family has a car the space serves many purposes. The motorbikes and helmets are stored here, so are our shoes. We put our laptops on the table and can talk to each other if we work or surf the net at home. There is a TV, an ironing board, a wardrobe and a bench that can be used as a bed. Raksmey sleeps here and there are floor mats and pillows for guests, but not for me.

Reaksa has one of the upstairs bedrooms, I have the other. They have prepared it for me.

The kitchen is behind the downstairs open space and behind that is a tiny backyard with a clothes line, a water tub and a high mesh fence for protection. Reaksa once bred guinea pigs in a cage here, but thieves climbed the fence and stole them. 'Be careful not to hang your tee-shirts too close to the fence, Yeay.'

Throughout the day the front roller door of our garage-like space is rolled up to let in the light and air. We hear the children calling to each other as they play in the street. Vendors pass our doorway selling food: bread, noodles and ice cream. The maze of streets is like a labyrinth; we can hear the special music of each vendor long before he reaches us. My favourite is the bread man who plays 'Amazing Grace' and carries warm loaves and baguettes in a covered basket on the back of his motor bike. I can smell the fragrance before he lifts the cloth.

My days in Phnom Penh settle to a predictable routine. Raksmey and I meet early each morning as he packs his bag, ready to travel across town to the Cambodian Development Research Institute. Reaksa takes me to the city on his way to university, and we meet to travel back again on his large red motor bike at the end of each day's work. We veer through traffic at sunset in a haze of petrol fumes, unlock the roller door and are glad to be home.

$$\Omega$$

It is lunch time in Proan Pra and midnight in Rochester Minnesota where the temperature is minus sixteen degrees. Snow is falling there. Reaksa and I have been watching a video clip of the energetic toddler Desmond Reaksa playing in the snow this very day. I hear his mother's voice telling him over and over that it is time to come inside but this little Cambodian boy in his padded snow clothes is reluctant. 'Mummy wants you inside now. That's a good boy. Come on now.' Srey Leak sounds firm and loving. As we talk about this her name flashes at the bottom of the computer screen. At last our times online match and we are connected to Skype.

Srey Leak has been out to dinner to celebrate her seventh wedding anniversary. Monee has returned from an event to raise funds for children in Cambodia and is ready for bed, warmly clad in a tracksuit and with her long hair loose below her shoulders. Srey Leak is walking around holding an iPad and showing me all the rooms of her new house. She and Siem have worked and saved to put a deposit on this home of their own. The little boy, 'Dizzy' they call him, comes sleepy from his bed and pats my face on his mother's iPad.

Reaksa has emailed the stories I have drafted. We talk of my writing and of Monee and her daughter's vivid memories of the past. Srey Leak says the word 'flashbacks'. I cannot tell whether she is talking of herself or of her mother or of the tight Cambodian community in Rochester. In all of my time spent with survivors this is the first time I have heard a Cambodian say these words. I have always known of the reality.

There is laughter coming to us across this great distance. Dizzy is growing more and more excited, rolling, tickling and giggling with his grandmother on the bed. I tell Srey Leak about my visit to Yeay in Battambang. We have all been worried about her eye operation but she now seems to be recovering.

Srey Leak is urging her father to come to Rochester for a holiday. She and Siem work hard for the life they are shaping but she could help with Nee's fare.

Ω

Reaksa cooks the evening meal, holding the preparation at just-before-ready, waiting for his father to arrive because Nee has sent an SMS that he looks forward to coming back from a week in distant villages and having a meal with us all. There will be special dishes tonight. Reaksa is considering studying to be a chef after he finishes his business management degree. I'm enjoying watching this young man, whom we called 'Lucky' at birth, sample the limitless options that seem to open before him. This January his hair is cut in a style popular among his friends at the university, shaved at the sides and back while ample and square at the top of his head. It took a few moments for me to recognise him at the airport.

We are hungry for hours but Nee hasn't come. Raksmey is keeping himself awake watching a Korean TV music channel while ironing shirts for himself and then for Nee. He finishes each carefully and hangs it on a rack. We remind each other that the bus from Battambang is often late. Past being hungry we now share disappointment.

Reaksa keeps checking the food on the stove, then goes out to the tiny backyard.

Tonight Nee's uncle, his mother's younger brother who still works as a motor-dup driver in Svey Reing, is with us. He is welcome to stay as there is always space for a mat on the floor.

It is well after ten o'clock. Just as we begin to worry that some accident may have happened on the risky road, the metal roller door rattles. Nee wheels his motorbike inside, takes off his helmet and has a word with each of us. He has brought home a packet of fresh meat and a bottle of Coca-Cola. I notice that he tries to do something thoughtful whenever some other responsibility has caused him to disappoint his sons. I wonder how it is for him to balance his sense of responsibility to those who still suffer, his realisation that he has authority to bring change and his need to be with those who love him the most. I wonder whether he realises that bringing home gifts doesn't compensate at all. Reaksa reattaches the gas to heat the meal then puts Nee's contribution away for tomorrow. Nee looks pale and tired but as he welcomes his uncle he tells him with a soft laugh that the meal will be 'part barang'. The old man nods knowingly. He has already steamed some rice in the pot and fried some small rice-field fish which he carried from Svey Reing, carefully packed in newspaper in his pocket. He is now ready for sleep.

We eat wearily, struggling to think of something to say. The special meal is flat with the waiting.

$$\Omega$$

It is hot in the small Proan Pra kitchen at the end of Raksmey's working week. I am glad to be here with him to listen to what has been happening at work; being part of the staff is very different from volunteering. Raksmey is washing dishes while I cook.

We talk about politics: the fifty-five opposition party candidates who were elected are still, after all these months, refusing to take their seats in parliament until the Cambodian Election Commission is reconstituted so that it is independent of the ruling party. They have not wavered though there is every financial inducement for them to take their seats. Raksmey has studied ethics and quotes from books he has read and lectures he heard at university. When we talk together like this I wish his father was here to listen to him; Raksmey has become a man while his father is busy with other things. In the past few years he has lost his lanky boyish look, his shoulders are broad, he has grown strong. It surprises me that suddenly we are talking as adults, discussing issues we both care about.

Our conversation stretches back to memories of twenty years ago. Then we talk of his father. Raksmey points to a large framed image of Nee on his graduation day at La Trobe University. It was, if my recollection is correct, taken from a phone camera and enlarged until blurry; there were surely better photos of his graduation than this. I am in the photo too. Raksmey says, 'Whenever we move house our father carries that picture separate from the luggage and puts it on the wall of our next house.' There is something important about his need to tell me this. I stop what I am doing and listen. Then he talks about a responsibility that he and Reaksa believe weighs heavily upon their father. They want me to tell Nee that there is no need for him ever to worry; they are ready to accept this responsibility when he can no longer do so.

'Raksmey, two or three years ago you told me that you understand your father better than he thinks you do.' He stands in the frame of the kitchen door opened to the cooler outside air. I look up at him as I speak; Raksmey is taller than I am. He looks to me, nodding. I take this as encouragement. 'What do you understand?'

He tells me. He went with Nee to a village and watched what happened there. He was amazed. There is something different about his father. Nee can change people's lives, people who are very poor. It is hard to explain. We both know that it is both a gift and a weight of responsibility that when Nee works with men and women who are without hope they gain dignity and are no longer passive. This is not so much something that his father chooses to do but rather something he must do.

WRITING FOR RAKSMEY

Raksmey has a circle of close friends. He shares meals, talks, and texts with them daily, but does not talk to them about his father. He expects they would ridicule a man with an overseas doctorate who missed the chance to take his family to a safe country. 'You went to Australia. You didn't stay!' people say.

'My father spends his life for strangers.' Is it hurt that I hear in Raksmey's voice? Insight? Both? I reflect, but do not say, that Nee will surely be forever bonded to those not yet free.

Sometimes Raksmey can cope with his father, sometimes he cannot cope at all. He knows what is happening, but he wishes it could be different. He and Reaksa try to care for Nee, Reaksa sending constant SMS messages, Raksmey stocking the kitchen with nourishing food when Nee is due to come home. They agree their father works far too hard, in addition to often working without payment. Sometimes they are completely frustrated. While Nee is in the village he forgets everything and everyone else in his life, and he will never learn to protect himself. He will speak 'soft words' to those who will, in the end, exploit his selflessness.

Nee's sons tell each other that when they expect Nee to be back in Phnom Penh on a certain date they should add at least a day or two in their minds.

'I know,' I say.

'We understand,' he says.

42

THE FARM

Nee knows that I want his advice about whether to seek a publisher for this manuscript I am working on. He is ready now to focus on what I have written. Before he turns the first page he advises that perhaps it should start with a chapter giving a sociological setting. I say I am choosing to write it as a story. He begins to read and his smile grows broader. 'Yes. Yes. Felt like that. Smelt like that.' He is nodding slowly to the words on the page.

I tell him about Raimond Gaita of Melbourne University, what he suffered in his life and the way he chose to tell it. I show Nee what Raimond Gaita wrote: 'I deliberately avoided anything that looked like theoretical descriptions and concepts … I did this because I wanted to convey in ways not obscured or softened by theory the full terribleness … while not diminishing the dignity of those who suffered it.'

Nee holds in both hands a printout of the draft I have given him. He nods. 'Thanks,' he says.

Ω

Nee and I sit on the veranda of the partly-built farmhouse. It has been a whirlwind journey by bus and motorbike for the chance to spend a day and a night here. Nee wants to do some ploughing; he also wants to show me his farm. I agreed to make the journey with him because it is almost time for me to return to Australia and if Nee really does settle on this farm I would like to be able to picture it.

I plan to walk around the two-hectare block, set in surrounding hills, where the light changes as the sun passes across the sky from sunrise to sunset, the quiet place where Nee dreams of spending the 'last part' of his life. This is where he can have time for thinking and writing and watching things grow, as well as for teaching. This, we both agree, is a good place for us to check the stories I have written.

It is night. Today the earth has been ploughed for the first time; there are fish in the pond. During the heat of the day there were no ripples on the surface though good fish food floated there. Small fish shelter under the shady bank while the sun is strong. Now that it is dark the surface is ringed with ripples.

There is a moon in the sky but it is not full enough for reading. We have a small solar light the size of a jam tin; it is sufficient for one person to see the printed pages. Nee asks me to read aloud those parts of the draft manuscript that tell his share of the story. It takes a long time.

We are there again, in the camp, in the gloomy early days of return, in the struggle to bring healing, to bring life. The night is quiet; the freshly-ploughed earth has a good smell.

Nee says 'Going back and remembering about these things is like coming through a dark tunnel. Each step comes from the step before.'

It is right that Raksmey and Srey Leak and Reaksa and one day the grandchildren should know all this, he says. Other people of good heart might understand these stories too. They need to be told. Publish them if you can.

We sit quietly, smelling the fresh earth, thinking of these things.

43

THE LIGHT SHINES THROUGH

Close to the monument for the King Father Sihanouk there is café where a new generation of Cambodian artists gathers. I am here to meet a sculptor, a Cambodian woman, whom I first met when she was sponsored to come to Melbourne.

It was a small gathering of people at Melbourne University, some who understood sculpture and some who knew Cambodia. I watched her come into a circle of light. She was clad in black cotton pyjamas, the uniform issued by the Khmer Rouge officials to their millions of slave labourers in the rice fields and digging gangs of the Pol Pot times. She carried in her two hands a terracotta cooking pot used in the villages to cook rice over a charcoal fire. She lifted the pot above her head like a consecration. She stretched out her hands and the pot shattered to the ground.

In the silence of those gathered around her she sat on the straw mat among the broken pieces, took a small tube of superglue from one pocket and a ball of string from the other. She gathered the large fragments and glued them, then, so that the glue would set, tied string around the skeleton of shape they made. She gathered small shards, pieced them together and pushed them into place. Nobody moved. Nobody spoke. It took an hour. Then she held it towards us saying nothing.

I talked to her there in Melbourne. We understood things that can be known but rarely put into words. She told me about a piece of art that she calls 'Broken' and invited me to see it in Phnom Penh.

As I wait for her my mobile rings. 'It's me. Nee. Just off the bus from Kompong Cham. Where are you? I can find a motor-dup and come to meet you.'

'Java Gallery. You know it? Yes, do come.'

Ω

There are thirty-three sheets of glass, each a sixty-centimetre square. Every square has been shattered then painstakingly glued together again: each sliver in place. Dangerous, meticulous work it must surely be. When set one upon another the pile of glass sheets is perhaps twelve centimetres in depth. A solid stack of glass squares. The light shines through.

Look at it from above. Layer upon layer of shattering and splintering. Layer upon layer upon layer of holding together. Broken edges in the top layer are clear to see. Lines are jagged. To gather sharp fragments and glue them in place must surely risk bloodshed. You notice first the patterns in the layers at the top. The layers at the bottom are harder to see. As you lean down to look you see the image of your own face.

Keep looking into the depth of it. It is luminous in the light. The more you relax the more you see. It is both fragile and strong. In the natural light the lines merge, glow, form a pattern, jade green now, a dense block of glass. It is beautiful. The strong lines in the top layer

THE LIGHT SHINES THROUGH

of glass merge into the fainter and fainter web of cracks in the depth. All is one: fragile and strong, broken and restored. The pieces are all there but nothing is the same as before.

I think of the poet Yeats who wrote, 'All is changed, changed utterly ... A terrible beauty is born'.

I tell Raksmey about it. 'Must be like a diamond when the light shines through,' he says.

SOURCES AND FURTHER READING

Multitudes of words have been written about the final third of the twentieth century in Cambodia, and about the start of the twenty-first. There is darkness and light. What I have retold from my journals and letters, what I have seen and heard, is one small piece of a complex mural.

Close to eight million people were taken captive when the Khmer Rouge seized power. Each was a witness, in their own way, to the 'Pol Pot Time' between April 1975 and January 1979.

Cambodian survivors' testimonies of this era, preserved in words on paper or on film, mostly come from men or women who found refuge in a safer country. Compared with the eight million, these permanent personal records are few.

The Khmer Rouge, during their days of unchallenged power, documented their deeds in unnerving detail.

In the years that followed, journalists, social and political commentators, activists and researchers recorded what they saw happening. Cambodians and foreigners reported on the seemingly unstoppable cycle of struggle, in the hope of bringing about change.

Some of the foreigners who worked in Cambodia during these years have written personal memoirs.

I have heard and seen far more than I have been able to write in this book. I know stories of Cambodians who stayed in their country throughout the long wars and the quest for peace. There are also stories of women and men who came from across the world and spent their years in Cambodia, to help restore a decent chance of life.

If my own years could be long enough there is much more I would want to relate and reflect upon. But I am already eighty years old. I pay tribute to all of those whose lives I have had the joy of sharing: lives of such deep tragedy and remarkable courage that they are surely worthy to be honoured.

Memoirs of Cambodians who survived Khmer Rouge times

Prahn, Dith, *Children of Cambodia's Killing Fields: Memoirs of Survivors*, Yale University Press, 1999.
Ung, Loung, *First They Killed My Father*, Harper Perennial, 2006.
Van den Berg, Jan, and Willem van de Put: *Deacon of Death: Looking for Justice in Today's Cambodia*, DRS Film and Buddhist Broadcasting Foundation, 2004.

Memoirs of foreigners who witnessed parts of this tragedy

Bizot, François, *Facing the Torturer: Inside the Mind of a Khmer Rouge Criminal*, Harper Collins Australia, 2012.
Bizot, François, *The Gate*, Harvill Press, 2003.
Dunlop, Nick, *The Lost Executioner: A Journey to the Heart of the Killing Fields*, Walker & Company, New York, 2005.

Contemporary accounts, reports and articles

Chantou B, Donovan P, Healy J, Kiernan B, Pilger J, 'Return to Year Zero', *New Internationalist* 242, April 1993.
Davenport, Paul, Joan Healy, and Kevin Malone, *Vulnerable in the Village: A Study of Returnees in Battambang Province, Cambodia, with a Focus on Strategies for the Landless*, Lutheran World Service, United Nations High Commission for Refugees, Japan Sotoshu Relief Committee, 1995.
Fawthrop, Tom and H Jarvis, *Getting Away with Genocide: Elusive Justice and the Khmer Rouge Tribunal*, UNSW Press, 2005.
Healy, Joan, 'Time for Cambodian Peace Ticking Away Fast' (essay written for UNTAC Battambang September 1992), *The Nation* (Bangkok), November 1992.

Human Rights Watch, 'Tell Them I Want to Kill Them', *Human Rights Watch Paper*, 3 November 2012.
Human Rights Watch, 'Cambodia: Stop Blocking Justice for Khmer Rouge Crimes', *Human Rights Watch Paper*, 22 March 2015.
Lynch, James F, 'Border Khmer: A Demographic Study of the Residents of Site 2 / Site II, Site B, and Site 8', Information Documentation, November 1989 (available at www.websitesrcg.com/border/camps/survey-1989.html).
Meas, Nee and Joan Healy, *Towards Restoring Life* (3rd edn), JSRC, Phnom Penh, 1996.
Meas, Nee and Joan Healy, *Towards Understanding: Cambodian Villages after War*, Josephite Publications, North Sydney, 2003.
Mysliwiec, Eva, *Punishing the Poor: The International Isolation of Kampuchea*, Oxfam, 1988.
Ponchaud, Francois, *Cambodia Year Zero*, Allen Lane, London, 1978.
Savin D, Sack W, Clarke G, Meas N, Im R, *A Study of Trauma in Site Two Refugee Camp*, American Academy of Child and Adolescent Psychiatry, 1993.
Simmons, M and Bottomley, R, *Working with the Very Poor: Reflections on the Krom Akphiwat Phum Experience*, Krom Akphiwat Phum, Phnom Penh, 2001.
Strangio, Sebastian, *Hun Sen's Cambodia*, Yale University Press, New England and London, 2014.

Scholarly research

Brinkley, Joel, *Cambodia's Curse: The Modern History of a Troubled Land*, Black Inc., Melbourne, 2011.
Chandler, David, *Facing Cambodia's Past*, Silkworm Books, Chiang Mai, 1998.
Chandler, David, *A History of Cambodia* (4th edn), Boulder, Westview Press, 2008.
Chandler, David, 'Songs at the Edge of the Forest', in Alexandra Kent and David Chandler, eds, *People of Virtue: Reconfiguring Religion, Power and Moral Order in Cambodia Today*, NIAS Publishing, 2008.
Etcherson, Craig, *After the Killing Fields: Lessons from the Cambodian Genocide*, Praeger Publishers 2005.
Hinton, Alex, 'Lessons from the Killing Fields of Cambodia – 30 Years On', *Christian Science Monitor*, 14 April 2005.
Hinton, Alex, *Why Did they Kill? Cambodia in the Shadow of Genocide*, University of California Press, 2005.

Osborne, Milton, *Southeast Asia: An Introductory History*, Allen and Unwin, 2013.
Sharp, Bruce, 'Counting Hell', Mekong Home Network (Cambodia Section), October 2008 (www.mekong.net/cambodia/deaths.htm).
Short, Philip, *Pol Pot: Anatomy of a Nightmare*, Henry Holt and Company, New York, 2000.
Taylor, Owen, and Ben Kiernan, 'Bombs over Cambodia: New Light on US Air War', *The Walrus* (Canada), October 2006.